Teaching

Obedience Classes

and Seminars

Joel M. McMains ———————————————

Howell Book House
New York

OTHER BOOKS BY JOEL M. MCMAINS

Dog Logic—Companion Obedience
Advanced Obedience—Easier Than You Think
Kennels and Kenneling
Dog Training Projects for Young People

Howell Book House
A Simon & Schuster Macmillan Company
1633 Broadway
New York, NY 10019

Library of Congress Cataloging-in-Publication Data available upon request.
ISBN 0-87605-470-X

Manufactured in the United States of America

10 9 8 7 6 5 4 3

Design by Lou Czar

One Wyoming winter night, two or three lifetimes ago, a cop friend and I were patrolling the county, talking away the boredom that is often the profession's signature. At one point my friend, who knew well my esteem for dogs, cut short my brilliant rechartering of the U.N. "Joel, have you ever thought about teaching obedience classes?"

I realized that I had, but only long enough to dismiss the notion. So we talked on the idea some, and some more the night after. Soon I enrolled my first student.

My friend was—is—James L. Robinson.

This book is dedicated to him.

I love in-seeing. Can you imagine with me how glorious it is to in-see, for example, a dog as one passes by. *In-see* (I don't mean in-spect, which is only a kind of human gymnastic, by means of which one immediately comes out again on the other side of the dog, regarding it merely, so to speak, as a window upon the humanity lying behind it), but to let oneself precisely in the dog's very center, the point from which it becomes a dog, the place in it where God, as it were, would have sat down for a long moment when the dog was finished, in order to watch it under the influence of its first embarrassments and inspirations and to know that it was good, that nothing was lacking, that it could not have been better made.

—Rainer Maria Rilke

Contents

Acknowledgments

A favorite author wrote that the acknowledgments page was the most important because the people named affected all the other pages. A keen insight, that, reminding me how surely I'm blessed by the friendship of Bud Swango, Ron Flath, Jo Sykes, Joyce Guerrero, Joanna Walker, Roger Davidson, Lawrence Zillmer, Carol Lea Benjamin, Rebecca Taylor, Nancy West, Susan Gauer, Susan Oard, Avril Roy-Smith, Ann and Jim McCammon, Karen White, Monika Mueller, Steve and Suzanne SeRine, John and Marilyn Thompson, Rudy Kasni, and most cherished, H. P. All have the uncommon ability to listen, and the even rarer gift for straight talk.

Seymour Weiss of Howell Book House: I owe you special gratitude for your continuing support and guidance in what I think of as the *Dog Logic* series. You and your people consistently fashion good manuscripts into better books.

Thank you, Doug Gundersen, for your photographic expertise, your artist's eyes, dedication and patience.

I also thank my students. They and their dogs have taught me much.

Preface

At some point in the career of most expert trainers, the question of teaching obedience classes comes to mind. However, many folks never take the idea further than thinking about it. Too often the allure of those ever-handy hidey holes, doubts and rationalizations, win out.

To wit: "Just because I can train dogs doesn't mean I can teach people."

Agreed, but neither does it mean you can't. Teaching isn't for everyone, and we'll explore that; but to say, "Maybe I can't" is also to say, "Maybe I can." "Maybe" means the speaker doesn't know and makes room for possibility. Once upon a time dog training was new to you, but what if you'd let hesitancy prevail when you were just learning how to hold a leash?

The reality is there's but one way to discover if you can instruct: Put your anxiety in a box, toss it into a corner, make a commitment to yourself and give teaching a try. Until you do you'll never know. Barring crystal balls or psychic hot lines, there's no way anyone could.

One thing is certain: Never giving teaching a shot is to risk missing out on an experiential dimension that is without parallel in the entire spectrum of working with dogs. As you know, a trained dog has a better chance at one permanent home for life, and that's the greatest contribution any instructor can ever make.

Trainers have much to offer by teaching. Most dog owners, let alone their pets, can profit greatly from professional training knowledge, insights and guidance. As understanding expands, appreciation grows and relationships deepen.

Another plus: Good trainers who teach become better ones. Instructors know what I'm talking about. If you've yet to begin or are just getting started, some joyous, enriching journeys are just ahead of you.

No, it's not all silk. Negatives prowl any path. But, like training dogs, teaching classes is miles past nine-to-five, time cards and company politics.

"A living can be earned teaching obedience classes?"

I manage.

Teaching Obedience Classes and Seminars illustrates how to teach, not how to train. But like my training books, this guide "offers concepts and techniques that may not be encountered elsewhere."[1] It presents "neither spoon-fed formulas nor a rehash of contemporary wisdom."[2] Underscore that with the presumption that anyone who would instruct is already a seasoned trainer and the message is "I'm writing to you, one dog-person to another, not to the dog-owning community at large."

As teaching is more profession than hobby, this book also covers advertising, organization, public relations, fee determinants, bookkeeping, forms, legalities, policy making, scheduling, class environments, sizes and groupings, assistants, problem solving and general business considerations.

Throughout these pages you'll encounter the terms "beginner" and "novice." As I use them they are interchangeable, referring to people and dogs new to obedience training. When alluding to CD (Companion Dog) competition, I employ the distinction "Novice." Further, "student" and "owner" denote the same individual, and "companion obedience," "basic obedience" and "novice obedience" refer to fundamental obedience training.

By design, the book is light on photographs. As I wrote in my proposal to Howell Book House, "My sense is trainers who would instruct don't need to be shown what a sitting dog or a leash looks like."

Finally, a suggestion. Whether you're a seasoned pro or are just getting started, be flexible, receptive. Keep an open mind. You may be surprised at the quality and quantity of lessons students and their dogs can teach you, provided they're allowed to. As Morris West wrote, "We are more readily betrayed by our certainties than by our curiosities."

---

[1] *Dog Logic—Companion Obedience*, xv.

[2] Ibid.

Part I

STARTUP

Chapter 1

PERSPECTIVES

FIRST LIGHT

Do you remember the first time you watched a trained dog? Not one who yawningly begrudged the handler a sit after umpteen commands, or responded accurately enough but who was nervous and hesitant, perhaps even fearful.

The animal I have in mind was a confident, eager, single-command worker who performed with smooth precision. His aspect spoke of desire, of purpose, and of fire. You may have found yourself thinking, I had no idea a dog could be taught such things.

Drift further into that memory and you may recall other impressions as awe-inspiring as the dog's feats: a sense that the animal's devotion to his human partner was total and unconditional; an aura that each was in tune with the other to the exclusion of all else on the planet.

During heeling they moved as one; during a stay the only distance between them was spatial. Handler and dog constantly yet effortlessly monitored the other's mood and feelings, as though a low-key energy hummed between them. They radiated the pleasure of each moment together, a pleasure beyond mere enjoyment.

Then perhaps you felt some inner stirrings, a few sparks began to flicker: "I wonder if I could train a dog like that? Fact is, I'd be happy if mine would just come when I call him. I sure wish I knew something about dog training, but I don't see how I could ever . . ."

For many of us, such thoughts constituted our world-of-dogs genesis, our point of origin, wondering if we could ever . . . That's also where many students start. Regarding dogs and training, beginners know little about either. Some folks are burdened by doubt: "I don't know if I can do this," and, "My dog isn't too bright."

Realizing that fledgling trainers often deal from insecurity, and acknowledging there was a time when you didn't know one end of a dog from the other, can make you a better instructor. It can take a part of you from where you now are to where your students are. It can lessen the distance between you.

STEP LIGHTLY

Distance is an obstacle inherent to learning. Not physical distance—obviously, teacher and students must be at the same place or there is no class. Distance as I mean it is a span of knowledge and experience: yours compared to a beginner's. You and I already know a great deal about dog training. We register details during a workout that the average novice wouldn't even notice. We reflexively do things that students have to stop and think about. You and I could discuss methods, techniques and implications for days but many newcomers couldn't even follow the conversation.

Communicating with students—not just tossing words into the air—requires that you bridge the knowledge gulf between you and them. You must perceive each person's level of understanding and build from that level; they certainly aren't ready to function at yours. Then, using empathy, interest, patience and a sense of "easy does it," you begin to guide, not to a destination (as some may think) but to a jumping-off point. You proceed slowly enough that all can keep up, but not tediously, lest they become bored. Once their journeys are well underway, and everyone is on secure footing, you begin to back away, allowing students the space to discover their own strengths and grow with them. You remain close enough for your help to be sought, but not so near as to stifle or limit.

Instructors who don't communicate at their students' levels of understanding, who have forgotten their own beginnings—who have not remembered the first time they saw a trained dog since the day of the event—accomplish little as teachers, and their students accomplish less.

NUTTY SOMETIMES, BUT OFTEN FULFILLING

Training dogs is easy and enjoyable. Doubtless that's why so many of us stay in the profession. Few careers exact so few demands while offering so much satisfaction. Though drawbacks attend any vocation, those of Obedience-class instruction are infrequent and minor while offering countless rewards.

Many good people and dogs come your way. Opportunities to witness, experience and contribute to growth occur as a byproduct. Your knowledge and awareness can expand; thoughts and ideas that may have long balanced on the edge of your consciousness may crystallize. Teaching opens doors—for instructors and students alike.

IMPETUS

Why are you drawn to teaching? What's your motivation? I hope it isn't to amass wealth. If so you are probably in the wrong business. In a good market, an instructor can derive a livable income, but I've yet to meet one whose earnings allowed for arriving at class in a chauffeured limousine.

Still, there's more than one measure of riches. If you enjoy working with groups of people and dogs, and if you take pleasure from watching them learn and grow together, teaching may be right up your alley.

REALITY CHECK

You're a trainer. You work directly with dogs. Entry into the world of teaching compels a paradigm shift. Your contact point becomes the owner, not the dog. I've known many patient, compassionate trainers who had difficulty abiding human foibles. While acceptance of human imperfection is somewhat optional for trainers, it's mandatory for instructors. A teacher who can't take folks as they are tends to judge people rather than abet their training efforts. Such a prideful attitude can so annoy owners that they become defensive, resulting in poor communication at best, an abbreviated teaching career at worst.

Another problem: Teaching humans requires more effort than training dogs. Contact is at once simpler yet trickier. While trainers must develop an interspecies language, instructors must master hopping from human-canine communication to that of human to human, and at translating either into the other. Though trainer and dog relate empathetically at an extrasensory level, a feeling level, the oldest and deepest form of exchange, interpersonal contact often necessitates degrees of posturing, game playing and "observing the amenities." Trainer and dog can be themselves together, unjudged, unlabeled, just accepted. Yet the very event of human meeting human can cause walls built of wariness to self-erect.

Trainers need but a "yes-no" decision point, while teachers must operate along a format of "yes-no-maybe-sometimes." This is because dogs perceive most situations in black-and-white fashion, but myriad gray areas exist in the scope of human relationships and understanding.

Other factors teachers must weigh are the topic under discussion; the student's knowledge of dogs and training; owner personality; predispositions and abilities; the level of bonding between human and dog; the owner's feelings for the animal; goals—the list continues, and each aspect must be evaluated before proceeding.

COROLLARY

No trainer can teach every dog, and no instructor can help every student. Like some dogs, some people are unreachable. To deny this is to set oneself up by courting an illusion.

Better a teacher *try* to reach every student, but without expecting to bat a thousand. Sound dogs are driven to learn. Perceiving the consequences of their undesirable behaviors, they choose a more advantageous path. People can't always do this. Those who decide to resist an instructor will do so. Such opposition is mercifully rare but it does occur. To maintain perspective you have to accept that when you've done what you can do, you've done what you can do. The alternative is to premeditate frustration.

Yes, once in awhile you may have to put your foot down, especially about subjects like class rules and mistreatment of dogs. But to do so reflexively about all topics is to reinforce and support inflexible thinking. When working with a head-in-the-sand student, though it may be easy to "put him in his place," the risk is he may turn his frustrations against his pooch. Thus, when confronted by obstinacy on two legs, put the dog's welfare first and hope the results achieved by those who follow your guidance will clarify the obvious.

PREDICAMENT

Some owners have the wrong dog, a situation over which you have no control. In extreme cases you may care to offer opinions but don't push. That can boomerang. The owner may know what has to happen but may not be ready to face it.

Your well-intended counsel can be seen as indicative of an interfering busybody, and later you may be cast the fall guy over a circumstance not of your making.

CRUX

Are you ready? Is your knowledge of dogs and training (and people) such that you feel you can handle anything that comes your way? Likely you're at that plane, else this book's title wouldn't have caught your interest. Still, the level that teachers should occupy is well said in the following quotation.

> There are attributes found in those special people called pros, the ones in the top 1 percent of their natural calling, attributes that redefine the word "excellence." The excellence at times approaches instinct, and at times the instinct approaches precognition. The "pro's pro" seems to be able to operate somewhere out front, two seconds into the future, two seconds ahead of reality. Awareness. The mind snapping a finished picture from a few starting details.[1]

STILL INTERESTED?

Now, have I talked you out of teaching Obedience classes? I hope not. That's certainly not my intent. In no way do I imply that working with owners isn't worth the occasional hassles. It is. Decidedly.

But as I wrote in the Preface, "Teaching isn't for everyone, and we'll explore that." This is what I've tried to do in the preceding pages.

The odds are that you and teaching will get along fine, but to assert that any skilled trainer would therefore be a good teacher is a non sequitur. I know some excellent trainers who would be terrible instructors. Totally at home with dogs, they possess scant patience with people, and are seldom at ease in groups larger than two (sometimes one). Most are wise enough to recognize this and to shun the idea of teaching. There's no disgrace in that. We all have limitations and comfort zones, and a wise soul respects and honors his or her gifts but does not push beyond his or her abilities.

A final consideration: Guard against letting externals impel you into uncomfortable situations. Peer pressure can lead folks into forgetting who they are by causing them to become obsessed with what they are not.

Whatever your decision, I wish you well.

---

[1] *Let Us Prey,* Bill Branon (New York: Harper Paperbacks, 1994), 257.

REFLECTION

How many men go to their graves without ever doing what's in their hearts?

—EMMETT ASHFORD

Chapter 2

SIMPLICITY

The title of this chapter pertains to matters like advertising, forms, record keeping and general business considerations. A principle applicable to each is that you'll get and keep more students by avoiding distractive clutter and detail.

ADVERTISING

An effective advertising medium is newspaper and shopping-guide classified sections. Radio and television are too expensive and generally ill-suited to our kind of enterprise. A person who might react to news of a sale at a well-known store may forget the phone number of a specialized business like a dog-training service before the next ad is finished.

The advertisement should be uncomplicated, containing only essential information. If too much material is presented, like starting dates, times, prices, minimum training age and so forth, you will lose potential students while increasing your advertising costs via the superfluous words. Many readers haven't decided to enroll, and an overly detailed ad can provide a list of excuses for not calling.

"It's too bad I'm going to be out of town when class starts." If this person had called you could have offered to arrange a private first session (assuming you're willing to do so), or noted the caller's name for the next series.

"My dog's too young—no sense in calling." If this owner had made contact, you could have kept his or her name on file for a subsequent class.

"Money's a little tight right now. They probably wouldn't let me pay in a couple of weeks." The heck I wouldn't, but first I have to hear from the individual.

I've used the following wording in regional classified sections for years. You are welcome to adapt it to your own needs.

DOG OBEDIENCE! Classes
offered by Joel McMains
starting soon.
Call 000-0000

Note the structure of this ad. Mentally remove the exclamation point and the first two lines read as a single sentence. That the elements are vertically linked on both sides of the center point is not happenstance. Reading downward, the service offered—the dog-obedience concept—is linked with my name and phone number. The same effect operates in "Classes offered" and "starting soon."

More conventionally, the first two words, in uppercase letters and bold type to catch the eye, tell what service is offered. **"DOG OBEDIENCE"** flows into "Classes" to capitalize on the fact that many people have heard of Obedience classes. The reader is then told via "starting soon" that there is still time to enroll but haste is called for. My name appears next, hopefully eliciting a favorable reaction: "Oh, yeah. I've heard of him." Lastly, the phone number follows the suggestion to "Call."

Applied to your service, this advertisement's wording also raises questions you alone can answer: When, where, how much, lessons covered and so on. The idea is to stimulate the reader's curiosity sufficiently so that he or she will call you. Understand: Advertising's function is not to sell your service. That's your job. An ad should cause your phone to ring. The rest is up to you.

An important advertising principle is continuity—keeping your name before the public. If you hold classes often, run your ad year-round. Start-and-stop advertising can suggest a hit-or-miss operation.

Proof all information the first time your ad runs. I know a lady whose advertisement contained an incorrect phone number, a lamentable fact she discovered only after several days of wondering why she wasn't receiving calls.

INFORMAL ADVERTISING

Another way to spread the word is to visit with local veterinarians, animal-shelter personnel, breeders, groomers and boarding-kennel operators. These people can do you a lot of good. Explain that you teach Obedience classes in the area and invite them to attend as observers (as your guests, of course).

BUSINESS CARDS

Have some business cards printed. Like your classified ad, keep your card simple yet eye-catching and informative. When calling upon local dog-business folks, ask to leave a supply for distribution among their clientele. A sample of my card appears below.

Obedience Classes

Joel M. McMains
K-9 Trainer

Phone (812) 299-2984

REFERRALS

A most powerful form of advertising is word of mouth. When I began teaching, most students heard about my service through classified ads. Today, over half of my new students are referred to me by former students, veterinarians, groomers and breeders.

After each novice first-class meeting, call and thank the folks who referred students to you. This simple courtesy takes little time, but the goodwill that can accrue is immeasurable.

HELP YOURSELF

Enhance your renown by participating in local dog-related activities: vaccination clinics, 4-H (or similar) dog projects, pet fairs, school demonstrations and AKC fun matches, to name but a few. Not only may you enjoy such events, taking part in community dog programs puts you more in the public eye while heightening your "dog person" status; it gets your name around.

ENROLLMENT FORM

That's what it should be called, not an "Application" form. The term *application* can subliminally imply a negative connotation: The student may not be accepted. *Enrollment,* on the other hand, is positive, sending a message of, "You're in."

The enrollment form should be worded simply, asking just for essential information. I've seen sign-up documents as detailed as governmental inquires, some seeming to border on invasion of privacy. A demanding form distracts from the business at hand, and implies a level of exactitude not appropriate to dog training. A sample form appears below.

[Name of Your Organization]

Obedience Class Enrollment

Please Print:

Owner's Name _____

Dog's Call Name _____

Age _____ Breed _____ Sex _____

Address _____

City _____ State _____ Zip _____

Telephone _____ Latest Vaccination Dates _____

Rabies _____ Distemper _____ Parvo _____

Kennel Cough _____

Have you trained a dog before? _____

How did you hear about these classes? _____

Agreement

I understand that attendance of a dog Obedience training class is not without risk to myself, to members of my family or guests who may attend, or to my dog(s), because some of the dogs to which I will be exposed may be difficult to control, and may be the cause of injury, even when handled with the greatest degree and amount of care.

I agree to hold the instructor(s) harmless for any claims for any loss or injury which may be alleged to have been caused directly or indirectly to any person or thing by the act of my dog while in or upon the training area, or near the entrance thereto, and I personally assume all responsibility and liability for any such claim; I further agree to hold the aforementioned party(ies) harmless for any claim for damage or injury to my dog, whether such loss, theft, disappearance, damage, or injury be caused or be alleged to be caused by the negligence of the aforementioned party, or by the negligence of any other person, or any other cause or causes. I further agree that this Agreement is binding for this and any subsequent classes that I attend.

_____

(Signature of Owner or Authorized Agent)   (Date)

Please make your check payable to: [**Name of Your Organization**]

Per the Agreement's last sentence, a student needs to fill out this form but once. There is no sense in requiring graduates of one level to complete an identical document should they enroll for subsequent instruction.

I require an Obedience Class Enrollment form and accompanying Agreement for each student and dog. If one individual enrolls two dogs, two separate forms are needed for legal protection.

BOOKKEEPING

Though a dog-training business seldom needs a complex accounting system, you should be able to substantiate all income and expenses. Columnar accounting sheets adapt well for recording transactions. Presented below are suggested column headings pertaining to income.

OBEDIENCE CLASS INCOME JOURNAL

DATE	STUDENT	AMOUNT	CLASS	EQUIP	TAX

Date	Transaction date
Student	Student's name
Amount	Amount received
Class	Class fees
Equip	Equipment sales (collars, leashes, etc.)
Tax	Sales tax collected, if any

Total the columns often, making sure that the *Class, Equipment* and *Tax* totals equal the *Amount* total.

The following headings pertain to expenses.

OBEDIENCE CLASS EXPENSE JOURNAL

DATE	CHECK#	TO/FOR	AMOUNT	ADS	OFFICE	RENT	EQUIP

Date	Transaction date
Check#	Check number; when using cash, write "Cash" in place of a number
To/For	From whom the purchase was made, and/or what it was for
Amount	Transaction amount
Ads	Advertising expense
Office	Costs of printed forms, postage and related items
Rent	Rental of a training site
Equip	Costs of collars, leashes and related items

The foregoing expense-classification headings are examples. You may need different groupings. Periodically verify that the totals of all expense categories equal the *Amount* total. Obtain receipts for all transactions. Facilitate expense tracking by writing the check number, date and amount on each receipt. File receipts alphabetically by vendor, and group those files by years for easier correlation to tax returns.

Using figures from the Income and the Expense journals, a summary report can be created. One format appears below.

OBEDIENCE CLASS FINANCIAL SUMMARY

	JAN	FEB	MAR	DEC	YEAR
Class Fees					
Equipment Sales					
Total Income					
Advertising					
Rent					
Office					
Cost of Sales					
Total Expense					
Net Gain/<Loss>					
Students					

Class Fees and Equipment Sales combine as Total Income. The sum of Advertising, Rent, Office and Cost of Sales yields Total Expense. Total Income minus Total Expense results in Net Gain/<Loss>. Amounts recorded in each Month column are totaled in the Year column. The Net Gain/<Loss> totals for each month should equal the Year Total Income minus Total Expense. The Students statistics track your business's growth. If you raise your prices, Total Income can mislead: Class Fees can increase though Students actually decreases.

RECEIPTS

Some folks request a receipt. Though blanks are available at most office-supply stores, you may be able to produce your own at less expense. A sample follows.

[Name of Your Organization]

Received From _____ Date _____

Amount _____ Dollars_____

Account Total $ _____ Payment For _____

Paid this Date $ _____

Balance Due $_____ Received By _____

DOES THE TAX MAN COMETH?

Equipment sales are likely subject to sales tax in your locale, but are instruction fees taxable? You're providing a service (as opposed to manufacturing or selling a product), and services are not taxable in many regions. Still, it is best to contact someone who knows (an accountant) and find out for sure.

LICENSES

You may need a business license and may be subject to other regulations. Some states, for instance, require that dog trainers who deal with the public be state approved. Do your homework on these and similar issues before opening your doors.

INSURANCE

If you can find affordable coverage you *may* be safer with it than without it. I stress "may" because my experience with insurance companies is that they honor only those obligations they cannot circumvent by whatever means.

Two scouting problems you may encounter are, first, many companies won't touch a business like a dog-training service, claiming it's too risky. Second, the premiums of those that will are often whimsical, to say the least.

REFLECTION

The great pleasure of a dog is that you may make a fool of yourself with him and not only will he not scold you, but he will make a fool of himself too.

—SAMUEL BUTLER

Chapter 3

BEFORE YOUR PHONE RINGS

You need to make several policy decisions before speaking with callers. Seldom can every eventuality be anticipated—culture, mores, population density and personal objectives are but a few factors that may influence your considerations— but every determination you make now saves an on-the-spot resolution later.

THE CLASS ENVIRONMENT

Indoors or out? That's the first question to answer. While climate and availability may make the decision for you, it's preferable to teach outdoors whenever possible. The dog who obeys outdoors will generally do so indoors, though the reverse is not always true.

An ideal outdoor training area is fenced to safeguard against dogs running away and to restrict intrusion. Not only might other animals wander into an unprotected area, possibly provoking a fight, but should a nonstudent enter the grounds and be bitten or otherwise injured, you could be open to a lawsuit.

A related consideration about where to hold classes is available parking space. There should be ample parking for as many vehicles as you have students.

Also, your training site should have a sign at the entrance: DOG TRAINING AREA—ENTER AT YOUR OWN RISK. Posting such a warning may not afford you a great deal of legal protection but, as an attorney once told me, "You may be safer with it than without it."

SCHEDULING

As top-of-the-hour times are easier to remember, especially when meetings are held weekly, schedule classes to start on the hour whenever possible. This isn't to say that starting on the half hour is necessarily problematic but avoid scheduling sessions at odd times, for instance 2:20 P.M.

A related thought: Plan classes not to conflict with popular national, regional or local events. I know of one training class that offered classes each fall on Monday evenings. Now, regardless of whether you're a "Monday-Night Football" fan, many people are; and it's just not shrewd to compete with an event having such a large, established following. To do so eliminates many potential customers, as the instructors discovered.

Though my competition-preparation meetings sometimes run longer, each of my companion, intermediate and advanced sessions lasts forty-five minutes to an hour.[1] Classes running longer than an hour, especially beginner sessions, tend to strain most folks' learning curve.

When scheduling several classes on the same night, allow adequate time between each for students to go and come without running into one another, and to give yourself a breather between sessions. You'll do a better job. Besides, it's not the problem of students in a fifth class that the instructor is worn out from teaching one class after another, nor should it be.

If you offer classes throughout the week, stagger the inception of each. That way you'll start new classes more often and lose fewer prospects who tire of waiting for your next series.

INSTRUCTOR ATTIRE

Regardless of climate or training environment, wear dense jeans or similar trousers to protect against scratches. Tennis shoes are preferable to heavy boots as they provide sure footing and less risk of injury if a paw is stepped upon.

---

[1] The first-week Companion-Obedience class sometimes runs slightly over an hour due to time needed for paperwork.

A cautionary note: Wear loose-fitting clothing. Should a dog bite, slack raiment gives better odds that the animal will snag garment rather than you. Also, regardless of weather, always bring a heavy, long-sleeved shirt or jacket. If you have to work a dog of size who tends to jump, donning such apparel can afford your arms some protection against potentially damaging nails.

CLASS SIZE

I limit classes to fifteen students. That's not to say I split a group should a sixteenth person enroll, but more than fifteen teams inhibit my ability to give personalized help. I could teach gatherings of thirty to forty—and do so at seminars—but at local classes I prefer fifteen or fewer students to ensure everyone gets the most out of their participation.

Safety is another factor. Fifteen untrained dogs can be risky enough; upwards of that many can be a disaster waiting to happen.

NO-SHOWS AND CLASS SIZE

My first-class no-show rate is very low, possibly because I contact all students a few days before the session and make certain each will be attending. Should I be hit with an unusually high no-show rate, I can usually find room in other classes for the students comprising the otherwise small group.

Another reason for staying with the not-more-than-fifteen concept is to facilitate getting an accurate reading on each dog and handler. That can be difficult enough when trying to keep an eye on fifteen duos.

The coin's other side is: How small a class is too small? The answer is entirely up to you. When establishing my business I taught classes of as few as three, as I knew that each satisfied student would send me many more.

CLASS GROUPINGS

I know instructors who group novice students based on the size of their dogs. Little dogs are trained in one class, medium-sized ones in another, large ones in a third, "Good Lords!" in a fourth. Several rationales are given but the one heard most often is safety: That it is thus impossible for a Mastiff to inhale a Yorkie, for instance.

If you prefer this approach, it's not my purpose to dissuade you, but I tend to mix 'em up, as it were, unconcerned if a class contains sizes ranging from the littlest littles to the biggest "Good Lords!" ever. I have several reasons for this policy.

First, let's revisit safety. To me, a uniform class can be chancier than a mixed one. Apply the fact that fighting can be contagious—one eruption can trigger another—to a grouping of fifteen large dogs. That's a riskier scenario than one having a sprinkling of big animals. Also, in a class consisting only of small dogs, owners may be less alert to potential trouble, reasoning that small dogs couldn't possibly be hot-headed.

Second: student convenience. I offer classes on weekday evenings and weekend afternoons. Many people not only have a preference for one slot over another, they simply can't attend certain meetings, due to business and professional obligations. Were I to arrange timetables according to dogs' sizes, I'd inconvenience many students and lose untold others since the times could easily be unsuitable for them.

Real-world training is intrinsic to my courses. Part of that philosophy acknowledges that dogs of all sizes may encounter one another beyond the classroom. While I outlaw canine contact at class, the animals do get to discover in a controlled setting that their genus comes in varying sizes. Though this is helpful for all concerned, it's more so for competition-oriented students: The optimum time for Miniature Pinschers to discover the existence of Borzois, and vice versa, is not during the group stays at a formal AKC Obedience trial.

Another consideration is student education. As you'll see in chapter 9, "First Week," I open my beginner classes by having students trying to identify every dog present according to breed. Enrollments grouped by size could make that a limited exercise.

Some students tend to compare their dogs with others, an unhealthy practice at best. In classes not grouped by size there is less of a tendency to do this as a more varied collection of animals is present. It's less likely that a class will be composed of similar-sized or same-breed animals, a grouping that would encourage inter- and intrabreed comparisons. Moreover, a class composed of a given breed could result in students comparing their dogs to a degree that could get downright irrational.

FEES

As class fees vary regionally, it's impossible for me to suggest what you should charge. Also, since you may not encounter this book until years after its publication, economic changes may render useless any price structure I might propose.

Thus, the best service I can offer is to provide considerations pertaining to how much to charge.

First, what are your expenses? You'll probably have advertising costs and may have to rent an appropriate space. Add in the outlay for other supplies, such as printed forms, transportation and so forth. Once you have an idea of what it costs you to put on a series, divide that amount by fifteen (or whatever number represents your maximum class size). The result is your cost per student. Then determine what you sense area residents will be willing to pay. The difference will be your profit, of course, and if you feel the amount adequately compensates your time, you're starting to get a notion of a workable price structure.

A second factor is the presence or absence of competition. If you have competitors, how good are they? I've known teachers for whom Daffy Duck would have been strong competition. They were able to stay in business only because no one else was offering local classes.

If you're just getting started, even though you feel you can offer a superior service, you may have to begin at a lesser rate than you think your services are worth. You would be ill-advised to charge more than the rates of established instructors. You're the new kid on the block, and to attract business you may have to appeal to owners' pocketbooks first. Lower rates are a quick way to turn heads. You can always raise your prices once you're established and have a solid, loyal following.

PAYABLE WHEN AND HOW?

I require total payment for my entire series at the first meeting. My purpose is to avoid extra bookkeeping, having to keep track of who owes me what. I've been known to accept half at the first class with the balance due in a week or so, but just in situations where my alternative was to lose a student altogether.

I don't accept credit card payments. That would increase my cost of doing business and add to my paperwork. To my knowledge I've never lost a student over my "Cash or Check Only" policy.

NO-SHOWS

Don't write off people who don't make it to a first session. Contact them to find out what happened. Students can fail to arrive for any number of reasons, and folks missing a first session may be hesitant to contact you. Call the students and, if you're willing, offer to catch them up privately. If nothing else, see if they'd like to be contacted prior to your next series.

Another reason for contacting no-shows is to make sure their first arrival isn't during your second session. It can happen. "We had unexpected company last week but we're here now." Now, there you are, ready to start a second-week class and you've got a student and a dog ready for a first-week class. Contacting no-shows after the first class avoids such dilemmas.

DROP-OUTS

This is a problem every instructor must face. After a few sessions someone doesn't show up, doesn't call, and you're left to wonder, What gives?

My suggestion is that you contact the truant and see what happened. That's just good business. It shows you're interested in your students and their dogs. Ask the individual if he or she has a problem with your class—you may learn something to improve it. Don't assume responsibility for another's decisions, however. Most folks who quit do so because they found there was some work involved, or because their motivation was lacking at the outset.

My drop-out rate fluctuates between 10 and 15 percent. Most who quit do so after the third class. I've found the general reason underlying these defections is that heel, lie down, stay and come have been covered by then, and that's all some people want their dogs to learn.

PHYSICAL LIMITATIONS

I wrote in *Dog Logic—Companion Obedience* that no one should own a dog whom he or she cannot physically control in a high-stress situation. To me that's just common sense. By the same token, I suggest you not enroll any dog you can't physically overpower should the need arise.

A seminar student once took issue with this point, asserting, "I think any professional trainer should be able to handle any dog." How the speaker arrived at this leap of logic I was not able to fathom. An extension of such reasoning would hold that any professional vocalist should be able to perform any style of singing, and somehow I have a little trouble imagining Willie Nelson performing grand opera.

The point is some dogs are physically too much for me and I know it. An on-the-fight, mature Saint Bernard heading in my direction will have this professional trainer scampering up a tall tree, preferably with a good book to read until the animal goes away. Some of the breed considerably outweigh me, and Saints can be quicker than some folks might believe. That makes for too much dog and not enough me. Should such an animal erupt and should the owner be unable to contain the situation, the word *catastrophe* springs prominently to mind.

TRAINING COLLARS

As readers of the *Dog Logic* series know, I prefer pinch collars. For many years I left the decision between choker and pincher up to each student. While this remains my policy vis-á-vis experienced trainers, beginners no longer have that option.

My motivation is essentially selfish: It's just too hard on me to watch abuse borne of ignorance in the hope that the student will someday perceive the obvious. I've seen dogs hit so hard with a choker that I wondered which would break first: The lead, the collar, the dog's spirit or his neck. I've also seen some of these same animals mercilessly beaten when they attempted to defend themselves by justifiably turning on the abuser.

Understand, I don't introduce pinch collars in a "Use this or get gone!" manner. I know how a beginner's first reaction could be, "But, I love my dog." I recall the first time I saw a pincher: I was nearly persuaded to ask the pet-shop owner to step outside and go a few rounds. Months later a kind, caring soul patiently showed me how a pinch collar is infinitely kinder than any choker, and I pulled my head out of the sand (or wherever I had it inserted).

As you'll see in chapter 9, "First Week," I confront the pinch-collar issue head-on but not in any sort of autocratic manner. Seldom do I encounter adamant refusal to at least try a pincher. When I do, however, I refund the fee and reduce my roster by one.

SWITCH

Occasionally you may have a student with, say, two dogs, who wants to enroll both but with the intent of bringing a different one each week. My response is to suggest the individual have a second person, preferably a family member, bring the second dog. This is done for two reasons. First, I know that both animals will be better trained if each participates in the entire series. Second, it increases my income, justly so.

If a caller can only afford to enroll one dog, I tend to go along with the two-dogs, one-fee request. Viewed from one perspective this costs me money, as I'm losing the income I'd receive for enrolling the second dog. From a more realistic standpoint, it would cost me more if I lost the student altogether. Also, under the heading of public relations, the situation occurs so infrequently that it's probably not worth risking the caller's ire by refusing the request.

Besides, it's the owner you're teaching, and so long as we're talking one person here, not two, what's the harm? Anyone can use the knowledge acquired at class to train other dogs at home. The only real difference is that another dog is at class every other week. You may not garner two fees, but that's preferable to no fee at all.

Similarly, when a student wants to enroll more than one dog, I sometimes reduce the price for the second animal, but only when I sense I'll otherwise lose the student's business and goodwill.

It's better to have a separate training class for youngsters, rather than include them in classes for adult students.

HOMO SAPIENS DIMINUTIVIS

Another question you'll be asked is whether you allow young people in your classes. I require students to be in their teens or older. My reasons are twofold: First, most preteens are inhibited when finding themselves in a group of adults. Second, in the event of a dogfight, all students must have enough maturity to quickly move their dogs (and themselves) from harm's way.

However, my thirteen-or-older rule doesn't always apply. If the youngster is, say, fifteen, but is incapable of handling his or her dog, safety considerations keep me from enrolling the team. In speaking with parents when they inquire about my classes, I give myself maneuvering room by saying, "I'll have to meet the child and the dog before I can tell you yes or no. Bring them to class and let's see what happens."

Be certain to have the youngsters' parents or legal guardian sign your Agreement (see chapter 2, "Simplicity"). A child's signature is legally meaningless.

Spectators, plural.

SPECTATORS

Except for folks I've invited, the only observers I allow are family or friends of enrolled students. Moreover, I encourage owners to bring family members so everyone concerned knows what's going on with pooch's training. To accommodate visitors I provide park benches in my training yard or folding chairs when teaching indoors. Children brought to class must remain quietly in one place, so as not to be disruptive.

REFRESHMENTS AND SUCH

I permit neither imbibing of "tall, cool ones" nor smoking during class. People are seldom inclined to drink or light up at class anyway, but the few times the subject has been raised I've kiboshed it. It's not a moral point, it's a training issue: Pursuing either habit during class is simply too distractive.

NO SHADES, EITHER

I discourage students from wearing dark glasses during training, except for individuals who need them to see properly.

Contact is a vital training concept and eye contact tops the list. A dog who can't see his owner's eyes will eventually quit trying to. He learns not to look your way, which is opposite of the attitude training is intended to foster.

WHOOPS!

When a dog fouls the training area, the owner should be responsible for cleanup. But rather than call undue attention to the event, thereby putting the student on the spot, point out during your opening remarks that you've provided scoops and a container for such incidents.

A related element is owner overreaction. Some folks exhibit untoward embarrassment over this kind of thing. You, however, must not allow the animal to be punished during a training class, verbally or physically, for doing what comes naturally. An owner who reacts inappropriately needs to be shown that reprimands would be proper only if pooch had been taught that your training area was off-limits. Otherwise, chastisement constitutes maltreatment, nothing more.

Watch for the owner who vainly tries to drag his or her pet from the training area while the animal is in mid-dump. Of course, all this does is scatter the leavings over a larger area. Have the person stand still until the event is passed.

ASSISTANTS

I don't have teaching assistants. Helpers with sign-ups and the like, yes, and thankfully so, but not teachers. To my way of thinking, if a person wishes to take a class from me, I'd be operating fraudulently were I to turn the individual over to an assistant. Such a strategy might temporarily swell my bank account but in the long run it could hinder my reputation.[2]

FIRST IN, LAST OUT

As you should be on site before students arrive, you should be the last to leave. This can be something of an inconvenience for you when several students wish to visit among themselves after class, but a worse situation is driving away, only to learn later that a student's car wouldn't start, and that he or she had to walk a goodly distance to find a telephone.

PUPPY CLASSES

I don't offer puppy classes. True, they're useful for socialization but that potential is offset by their inherent potential for spreading disease.

Besides, puppyhood is a most special time, and a dog can be trained quickly and easily enough when he's more mature. My feeling is, What's the rush? Let a puppy be a puppy.

This doesn't mean a young dog can't be taught housebreaking, not to jump on people, and not to zap the family cat. But formal Obedience lessons during the stage of a two-second attention span can be a spirit breaker.

In training terms, puppy classes can be detrimental to long-range goals. Consider that in many classes a pup is shown that he may ignore "Sit," for example, as no serious enforcement is used. This is as it should be, as no puppy should be pressured—force can frighten a puppy at an age when he's emotionally vulnerable. But it's equally true that no dog should ever be taught that a command allows a choice, especially during the impressionable phase of puppyhood. Thus, trouble can develop in that, while "Sit" doesn't mean "Smack your butt on the ground, then hop up and do whatever you please," without enforcement that's how a puppy typically responds when commanded to sit, especially among peers.

When that fact is pointed out, puppy-class advocates often worsen a bad situation by contending that corrections—force—are added to the program when

---

[2]A legitimate exception to "No Teaching Assistants" occurs with handicapped instructors. See the section entitled "Should an Impaired Individual . . ." in chapter 16, "Impaired Owners."

pooch is old enough to handle them. That's mixed signals. Demonstrating initially that commands are open to a vote and then later changing the rules is an excellent way to instill confusion and distrust in any animal.

A second problem concerns trainer attitude. A professed puppy-class aim is to demonstrate that Obedience is a fun and pleasant activity. That's a valid sentiment, but I've known its expression to have a boomerang effect: Some novices come away with the erroneous impression that when serious teaching is commenced, the "fun and pleasant" element is no longer appropriate as the animal is no longer a puppy. Owners may not consciously reach that conclusion but I've seen the effect. Of course, a positive attitude should be constant in any training program, regardless of a dog's age.

PUPPY SOCIALIZATION

You may be asked if puppies can be brought to your regular meetings for socialization purposes. I allow it, but not unconditionally. Puppies must be on-leash, supervised, and must be prevented from contacting other dogs. Puppies, even those who have been started on their vaccinations, are highly susceptible to disease. Also, a puppy who sniffs the wrong dog could be snapped at or even bitten, which could physically or emotionally scar the youngster for life.

REFLECTION

It would be a much better world I suspect if we didn't try to draw a distinct line between ourselves and the "lower animals," whatever they are, a distinction made in hell that serves no good purpose, just a whole bunch of bad ones.

—ROGER A. CARAS

Chapter 4

INQUIRY

"I'd like information about your Obedience classes."

Expect calls between early morning and late evening any day of the week. The training-classes business is like that. Though Obedience-class enrollment sometimes results from an owner's careful planning, more often the caller is acting on impulse. Often he or she has grown fed up with pooch's unruly antics, or has heard about your service and is responding out of curiosity.

In any case, allow the caller to set the inquiry's duration. You'll be able to deal with most individuals in a matter of minutes. Some folks, however, are going to want to talk your ear off and that, too, goes with the territory.

Early in the conversation I ask, "What kind of dog do you have?" Then, "How old?" Some people are unaware of Obedience training's elements, to the point that they don't know what to ask. Since most folks are comfortable talking about their pets, these questions ease callers into a familiar area. Pretty soon we're chatting away, the prospect is at ease, volunteering details about pooch's behavior without my having to assume an interrogative role, and he or she is more receptive to new concepts. Assuming the person decides to enroll, I record pertinent details on the following form, and advise that I'll reconfirm the starting date a few days before the first class.

Students enroll in Obedience classes with many different objectives in mind.

```
OBEDIENCE CLASS INQUIRY

Date _____

Name _____ Telephone _____

Breed—Dog #1 _____ Age _____ Gender _____

Breed—Dog #2 _____ Age _____ Gender _____

Referred by_____
```

Checklist:

☐ Friendly ☐ Shots ☐ Day, date, time

☐ Duration ☐ Cost and terms ☐ Equipment

☐ Location ☐ Directions ☐ Don't feed

☐ On-leash ☐ Walk around ☐ No sniffing

☐ If canceled

```
Notes:_____

_____

_____
```

The Checklist segment above serves as a reminder to cover routine information with each caller.

Friendly: Is the dog manageable? I don't accept chronic hotheads, nor should you.

Shots: The animal must be currently inoculated for rabies, parvo, distemper, kennel cough and any contagious diseases endemic to your local area.

Day, date, time: When the class will meet.

Duration: The series runs five weeks; each weekly session lasts from forty-five minutes to an hour.

Cost and terms: The fee per dog/handler team, payable at the first class.

Equipment: The type of leash and collar required.

Location: The class site.

Directions: How to find the training location.

Don't feed: I tell callers not to feed their pets within six hours of class, to lessen the chance a dog might foul the training site.

On-leash: Pooch must be on-lead before exiting the vehicle.

Walk around: Pets must be walked well away from the meeting area before entering, to lessen chances of fouling.

No sniffing: No dog may sniff another, the idea being to prevent dogfights or disease transmission.

If canceled: I call students one hour before a scheduled class if it's canceled, as can happen with outdoor sessions during inclement weather. I advise students that if they haven't heard from me by an hour before class, "Class is on!" This policy is to keep my phone from ringing off the hook on cloudy days.

Observe that I don't have a note about student attire on the checklist. This is because I've observed that most folks don't need to be told what to wear to an Obedience class. Should someone arrive in swim trunks or evening gown, I have a private word with the individual.

WAITING LISTS AND FOLLOW-UPS

With owners of pets too young for an upcoming series I offer to "take your name and phone number and call you when the class your dog should be in will get underway." I also tell callers, "If you have any problems with the puppy in the meantime, give me a call." This shows I'm interested, am willing to help and want the person's business. I then record the information from the Obedience Class Inquiry form onto a list having the following headings.

MONTH—YEAR				
STUDENT'S NAME	PHONE	BREED	AGE	NOTES
_____	_____	_____	_____	_____
_____	_____	_____	_____	_____
_____	_____	_____	_____	_____
_____	_____	_____	_____	_____
_____	_____	_____	_____	_____
_____	_____	_____	_____	_____

Five days before a scheduled series I call each student, confirm that he or she is still interested, repeat the "when" and "where" elements, and review other sections of my checklist as needed. If I detect indecision, I don't push but do explain that I need to know the individual's intentions as space is limited.

There are two reasons for the five-day interval. First, people need time to meld the class into their schedules. Second, when teaching outdoor classes, I avail myself of the weather bureau's five-day forecast. If the agency's prognostication is "a 100 percent chance of major precipitation," I delay starting the opening session until the following week. There's no sense in lining up a series only to have to cancel.

WHEN YOU AREN'T HOME

A phone-answering machine can pay for itself by recording one call you would have otherwise missed. Of course, your answering message should never be cold or aloof but should be brief, businesslike and to the point. A long, rambling message or one with idiotic sound effects can lose callers; many people don't have the patience to sit through an infantile or hard-on-the-ears recording.

MORE ABOUT TELEPHONES

Do you need a separate line? Consider that phone companies charge more for business service than for residential lines. If you have talkative teenagers, or if there are other reasons why your phone might often be busy, the increased cost of a second line might be money well spent. Customers don't like to encounter a perpetual busy signal, and may decide to solve the problem by calling another instructor.

SCHOOL AGE

The call that never fails to tickle me is from the owner whose pup is eight or ten weeks old, and who's been told that this is the perfect age to initiate formal training. More than once I've heard a gasp when I advise it's a mistake to begin sooner than at six months.

Starting too soon risks frightening the pup. Puppies are very impressionable, and the little one could learn to fear collars, leashes, or—God forbid—you. Training too young can produce obedience but for all the wrong reasons.

"But, my brother-in-law, Leroy, he told me . . . ," and I imagine you can fill in the rest. A temptation may be to suggest that Leroy train the dog, but don't succumb to the urge, if for no other reason than the caller might take you up on it. Not only would you lose a student, the dog would lose the opportunity to have an educated owner. It's better to let the caller have his or her say and then gently point out that while Leroy may indeed have trained his own dog, you train professionally, and are better qualified to assess minimum training age.

"MY DOG IS METHUSELAH"

That's the flip side. While I don't have a carved-in-stone maximum cutoff age, once a dog is beyond nine or ten years it's not only a bit late to try turning him around, it's unfair. By then the animal is too set in his ways to reverse a lifetime of learning. He can be shown a few basics, and problem behaviors can be lessened, but precision shouldn't be a goal.

When callers ask, "How old is too old?" generally they are concerned with ages ranging from one to four years. Someone has told them that their dog's age makes the situation hopeless and, not being trainers, they believe it. The truth is that I've worked with five-year-olds who absorbed lessons like a sponge.

CALLERS SOMETIMES ASK . . .

Q. "Can I observe a class before enrolling?"

A. "Sure, but I have to ask that you leave your pet at home; I only allow en-rolled dogs at the training site. You and I can visit after class and see what you think."[1]

Q. "Do you teach how to teach classes?"

A. "By example, every time I run a series."

Q. "How many class series would I have to attend to learn how to teach Obedience classes?"

A. "That depends on your background and experience. If you've trained dogs for several years, a dozen or so series should have you fairly comfortable."

Q. "Can I bring food to reward my dog with?"

A. "Sure, but hold off using it until we're through the second class." I want the owner's praise to come to be the reward, but this person isn't far enough along in training comprehension to see that. Hence I deflect the request, hoping the individual will have gleaned enough from two classes to understand and ap-preciate the power of praise.

Q. "I've trained many dogs and have my own methods. May I attend your class to work my dog around other animals?"

A. You'll seldom be asked this one but often enough that it's worth ponder-ing beforehand. Most "I've trained before" callers realize they can't be part of a class and independent of it at the same time. Many will give your training meth-ods a chance as they'll see an opportunity for learning. As long as the caller is open-minded, I honor such requests.

Q. "My dog's not too bright. What if he doesn't learn anything?"

A. "Dogs who complete my class can be taken through again by the same owner at no additional charge." This has been my policy for years because, first, I don't want anyone to come away empty-handed, feeling that his or her pet didn't learn anything. Not only might the student vilify my name among his or her friends, I like to feel I earn my fees. Second, callers who say their dogs are "five-watters" are often indicating self-doubts, and telling them that pooch can repeat at no cost seems to remove enough stress for them to give the class a try.

---

[1]Require that observers sign your Standard Agreement (see chapter 2, "Simplicity").

Q. "Will I have to be mean to my dog?"

A. When you hear any variation on that question be very careful—one wrong word is all it may take to lose this caller. You and I know that a trainer must be one inch tougher than the dog (else the animal trains the owner), but now is not the time to discuss training ideology. Somewhere along the way this individual has perhaps had a negative training experience, misperceives its function, needs your help and may be a candidate for observing a class before enrolling.

When I've encountered this type of nervous hesitancy, in each and every case the people not only developed into competent trainers, they became some of my more ardent supporters and promoters. Word of mouth goes a long way in this business; the direction it takes is up to you.

And by the way, the answer to the caller's question about being "mean" to pooch is, "Of course not."

TRAINING EQUIPMENT

To arrive at a first-week novice class, each team needs a six-foot leash and a properly-sized choke collar, nothing more. In time students will need a fifteen- to twenty-foot leash but there's no pressing need for one yet.

Though I prefer leather leads, they are expensive and not always easily obtainable by the average pet owner. I recommend leather leads to callers but I point out that nylon or pressed-cotton leads—except for the largest, most powerful dogs—will serve the purpose.

The leads I discourage are chain leads and retractable types. Chain leads are heavy, not to mention noisy and rough on a trainer's hands and legs. Retractable leashes are not only easily broken, they're too clumsy for effective handling.

You've noticed I tell callers they need a choke collar. Readers familiar with my training methods know I favor pinch collars. However, that topic is better delayed until the first meeting. Mention the pinch-collar concept on the phone and—regardless of your eloquence in stating your case—half of the students won't show up. The look of the collar puts them off. Pinchers are best introduced when you can immediately demonstrate their effectiveness, along with the fact that they won't "hurt" (as in "injure") anyone's pet. Hence, the recommended "properly-sized choke collar" is to create a safer environment, each dog wearing a collar that affords some measure of control and is unlikely to slip off.

EQUIPMENT SALES

A related consideration is whether you want to get into the leash-and-collar business; Do you want to go retail? I sell pinch collars but I buy from local suppliers. This reduces my per-sale profit as I could get collars cheaper through catalog houses, but it's not smart to compete with local businesses who may send students my way.

Besides, I'm not trying to get well on sales anyway. I sell pinchers to ensure each dog's collar is of the proper weight and is correctly sized.

REFLECTION

A wise man is favourably disposed to a dog which is well brought up.

—W. W. GOETHE

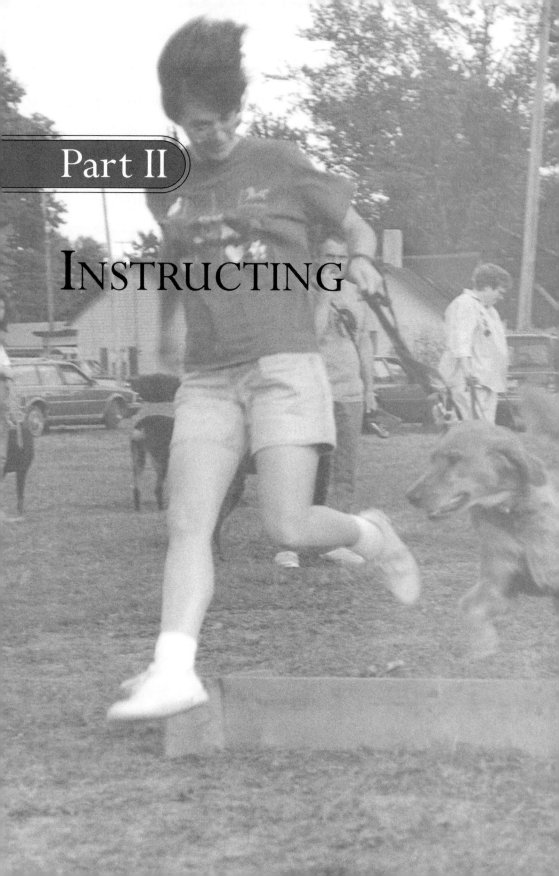

Part II

INSTRUCTING

Chapter 5

TEACHING GUIDELINES

THEME

Like my approach to training, my teaching philosophy strays from convention. Experienced hands will note examples throughout the instructional sections, not just in the lessons presented but in the perspective from which they're offered.

One primary divergence—one that may prompt outcries of "Heresy!"—needs to be stated outright: My beginner series is not predicated upon the AKC Companion Dog routine. Sits, downs, comes, heeling and stays all grace my curriculum, yes, but for their intrinsic worth, not because they are CD elements. I accent training's practical applications, not its competition potential.

Excluded from my basic classes are the figure eight and the stand for examination. Stays are seldom practiced in straight-line groupings and if someone in one of my classes wants pooch to heel on the right, that's fine with this instructor.

Why this separation from the commonplace? To satisfy the wants of most students and ensure they get their money's worth. Fact: Rare is the newcomer who enrolls to learn about showing. Sure, it happens occasionally but most dog owners are pet owners who have neither the time, interest nor inclination for competition. They want obedience suited to the way they live. Period.

Consider a few specifics. I said I don't teach the figure eight, but my students do practice heeling in far more distractive pedestrian-traffic settings. While the stand for examination is pointless in real-world terms, I teach a stand-stay to facilitate handling a dog during grooming sessions. Sit- and down-stays are practiced with dogs scattered about while students visit with one another, not ring-style with owners stationary, several feet from and staring at their pets.

The key phrase is "real-world." That's where most people live, and what they want is around-the-house, take-the-dog-for-a-walk obedience. Further, I encourage students to be mutually supportive; infusing competition can pit them against one another. It also can make unfair demands upon the majority and it is they, after all, who pay most of the freight.

Consider a related point. Just as a dog can be taught too much at once, students—especially those new to training—can only handle so much at a time. As any exhibitor can attest, there's a vast difference between house-pet obedience and competition training. To expect amateurs to learn simultaneously the concepts of Obedience training and showing is not only too rigorous, it denigrates competition.

Besides, people want to have fun training their pets, and rightly so. They don't enroll to be drilled. To couch explanations along a reverberating theme of, "Because the AKC requires it," and cram ring requirements down unwilling throats is to risk alienation. The effect can be the reverse of that intended by instructors wishing to turn folks on to competition.

There is also a pragmatic consideration in offering noncompetition basic classes and requiring all first-time students start there. It allows winnowing of those who have the ability and interest—and who have the dogs—for subsequent enrollment in competition courses. This not only matches competition-oriented students with their desires while satisfying everyone else, it has the salutary effect of augmenting the teacher's income while ensuring that competitors' pets will be well schooled in the basics.

EASY DOES IT

Good instructors come across in relaxed fashion. It's an infectious attitude, one that students often catch and send along the leash, making learning easier for people and dogs alike.

A side effect is to demystify the training process. To you and me there's nothing complex about training anyway, but there'd be little need for our services if beginners shared that perception. Many people arrive at class clueless about how to communicate with their pets. Some knew how as children, but misplaced that knowledge along the road to adulthood.

A style characteristic of the "relaxed-fashion" instructor is the illusion of ad-libbing the presentation, of just letting it flow. The reality is the teacher knows exactly where his or her classes are going. The instructional style is just a way to get there while helping owners be at ease.

SO DON'T WING IT . . .

Plan each lesson carefully. Examine every move you make when teaching a dog a lesson so you can be sure to tell students what they need to know. You may discover you're so familiar with some aspects of technique that you've forgotten you know them; they've become reflexive.

. . . EXCEPT WHEN YOU SHOULD WING IT

In the course of most novice series I teach *Resistance Stays* and *Reversed Heeling*.[1] With some few groups, however, I skip the techniques as they are more than the students can handle. That's what I mean about winging it.

NOTES

If you prefer to teach from notes, confine their length to what can be written on a three-by-five card. To operate from several sheets of paper can suggest that you don't know your material. Students may lose confidence in you, which can lessen their optimism about what they may achieve through your class.

JAMMED CIRCUITS

Present limited amounts of information at a time. Hit the high points but don't worry about intricacies that might appeal to advanced students but are too much for beginners. Remember that anyone's mental receivers/interpreters can shut down when besieged by too much input. If you see glazed eyes or blank looks, back off. You can always cover more another time.

---

[1]Both techniques appear in *Dog Logic—Companion Obedience.*

DON'T GET STALE

Whatever you tell students will be old material to you but new and fresh to them. Keep your presentations that way. Sure, this afternoon may mark the zillionth time you've shown a group how to teach, "Sit." For your current class, however, it's a brand-new day.

TIMING AS A FACTOR

After making a major point, pause for few seconds to allow time for your message to sink in. I've attended sessions, principally seminars, where the instructor's delivery was not unlike an auctioneer's, and how anyone was able to digest the material I could not imagine.

VOLUME AND ACOUSTICS

Speak loudly enough to be heard clearly over the whole area. Some students will say, "I can't hear you," but many won't.

At the same time, don't knock students down with volume. Excessive decibels can inhibit.

Keep in mind that parts of creating an optimum volume level relate to where you position yourself relative to your students, and whether your classes are indoors or out. When working inside, use the building's acoustics to everyone's advantage. When outside, try to keep any wind at your back to carry sound better, and position yourself so students don't have to squint into the sun to look at you.

CLARITY

Break lessons into steps, then summarize those steps. People often better remember lessons given in one-two-three (four-five, and so on) fashion. Using "Platz" ("Lie down") as an example, I teach as follows.

With your dog sitting at heel:

One, kneel next to him;

Two, command "Platz" while patting the ground;

Three, guide pooch into the down position;

Four, praise "Good Platz."

Kneel, command while patting, guide, praise.

Another clarity issue pertains to word choice. I once referred to a student's "Rotty cross," as in *crossbreed*. The owner thought I meant her dog was angry.

BREVITY

Use short sentences. In the "Platz" example above, the longest sentence contains seven words. The second step could be, "two, command 'Platz' and pat the ground in front of your dog, to give him the idea of what you want." But since I accompany the lesson with demonstration, the words "in front of your dog, to give him the idea of what you want," would be wasted. Students can see where and why I'm patting the ground.

FRANKNESS, NOT FOLDEROL

Subtlety is sometimes useful but in most situations be direct and clear. During heeling practice, for example, when you want students to run, say so. Don't use the vague AKC Obedience directive, "Fast!" Say, "Run!"

Refrain from buzzword terminology, especially when teaching beginners. Use everyday speech. Using unfamiliar terms is akin to speaking in a foreign language: Listeners won't—can't—understand what's being said. The result is not only confusion but increased distance: In-crowd jargon can make students feel left out.

Similarly, don't attempt to plumb complex conceptual depths, especially during basic classes. Explain both the whys and the whats, and answer all questions, but keep your messages at a familiar level that people can handle. Students learning to count aren't ready for differential calculus.

Stick with concrete lessons and examples. Don't dwell upon theories or abstractions, especially when working with youngsters. Successful communication via abstract concepts often hinges on common experiences and common perceptions. Theories can be useful when working with experienced trainers, but high-powered concepts can confuse or mislead novices.

FEEDBACK

Because students are at a disadvantage—you know what's going on, they don't—some may act as though they understand everything you're saying when in truth they haven't a glimmer. They do this to be polite and to avoid drawing attention to themselves by asking questions, lest other students think them dim. It's one of many negative carryover effects of institutionalized, force-fed learning. Make sure your message is getting through by asking students to explain it back to you.

ADVANCEMENT RATE

Teach at a pace the class can handle. Sure, you may be able to take advanced trainers through a Utility exercise in two or three minutes, but novices may need twice that time to internalize a basic. For instance, you and I know how easily and quickly a finish can be taught, but a beginner first seeing the exercise can feel overwhelmed.

"WE DID IT!"

It is vital during beginner classes that you format lessons so students can rapidly achieve success. As much as students need knowledge, they need confidence. If they believe they can train their dogs, they probably will; but if they feel they can't, they surely won't. It's that simple.

Sure, some things take time to polish, but an overall sense of having quickly accomplished something builds self-assurance. That raises the odds for success. If you yourself achieve rapid results with a problem dog, point out that you have several years experience—"If I can't make it look easy by now, I'm probably in the wrong business"—and remember there was a time when you were just learning, too.

THE "HOW COME?" FACTOR

Encourage students to use their minds. Show them there are reasons why training techniques do or don't work. Introduce the concept of how to "think dog."

For instance, one insight I give students is presented as a question: "Do dogs perceive sitting as an action or a body position?" (See chapter 12, "Fourth Week," for the answer.)

Along similar lines, when someone is having difficulty, don't reflexively state what's being done incorrectly. Ask the student what he or she thinks the problem is. When an instructor guides rather than prescribes, very often the owner leads him- or herself to the answer. This results in stronger learning since later the student doesn't have to remember what you said. He or she can lead him- or herself to the answer again.

"SHOW ME"

When a student reports a training difficulty—"When I tell my dog to . . . he tends to . . ."—your response should be "Show me." In other words, don't draw conclusions from a student's description of a problem; have the person demonstrate it for you. Why? Because what a student thinks he or she is seeing may not be what is actually occurring.

SUPPORT

If you sense that a hesitant student knows or can do a given thing, let him or her know it, too. People often respond as expected, so "Sure you can," is far more helpful than, "You'll get it eventually."

Likewise, if someone tries to answer a question, however accurately, "You're real close" encourages, while "No, that's not right" slams the door on the student's initiative. Don't patronize by saying that something is well done or correct when it isn't, but pick out and accent the positive aspects inherent to most circumstances.

OVER AND OVER AND OVER AND OVER AND . . .

Repetition can be useful but monotony has no place in teaching. Tell students a given thing once; then see if it took. When you do repeat a point, shade it in a somewhat different light, saying the same thing but differently. To expect to overcome faulty communication by repeating oneself verbatim brings to mind a friend's definition of insanity: doing the same thing and expecting different results.

STUDENTS CAN TEACH

Students' observations about each others' performances are very helpful. For instance, a few weeks after introducing heeling, have each team briefly heel while the others watch. Then ask everyone what they saw. This not only provides important feedback, watchers become more aware of what they themselves have learned.

FOR LATER REFERENCE

Written handouts enable students to reexamine material covered during class. After distributing weekly summary sheets, review them. People often learn better when a written guide is covered verbally. You needn't read entire outlines aloud but make sure everyone understands the gist.

Regarding appearance, my forms are headed as follows.

Joel M. McMains

(Level) Obedience Training

(Level) denotes the class as Companion, Intermediate or Advanced. The synopses for the first two weeks of the Companion Obedience class appear below.

OBEDIENCE I
WEEK 1

Training Exercise	Command	Per Session	Foundational or 7-Day Objective
1. Heel On-Leash w/Automatic Sit	Fuss (Heel)	8 to 15	Dog's attention & comprehension
2. Sit-Stay	Stay	3 to 5	6 feet - 1 minute

OBEDIENCE I
WEEK 2

Training Exercise	Command	Per Session	Foundational or 7-Day Objective
1. Heel On-Leash w/Automatic Sit	Fuss	As Needed	Dog's attention w/ distractions
2. Sit-Stay	Stay	2 to 4	15 feet - 2 minutes
3. Down-Stay	Platz/Stay	4 to 6	15 feet - 2 minutes

As suggested by the preceding "Week 2" summary, new lessons and objectives, and changes in prior ones, such as stays becoming longer in time and distance, are incorporated into the list.

Brief descriptions of each exercise's training technique follows the boxed material. Each sheet also contains the following footer, which includes the page number (indicated by the WordPerfect 5.1 computer code, ^B).

Training•Classes•Seminars•Howell Care & Training Texts

Page ^B

Along with lesson sheets, at initial Companion-Obedience meetings I distribute two other forms: *Companion Obedience* and *Training Hints*. *Companion Obedience* covers class information and rules, such as, "Please, *never* bring a sick dog to class, especially one with an excessive, prolonged cough." *Training Hints* offers general guidelines, like, "Praise calmly and quietly, communicating approval rather than affection. Affection is bound to creep into the process but it should be given to a dog throughout his life—he shouldn't have to work for it."

BUILDING BLOCKS

Be sure to practice all previous weeks' lessons at subsequent classes. "That's obvious," you may say, and I agree it should be, yet I've known instructors to teach a given exercise and not refer to it again.

DEMONSTRATE AND EXPLAIN

These points are evident too, but they must be expressed: Describing is important but demonstrating is essential. For example, heeling can be verbally characterized but much more is accomplished by showing heeling in action.

Link your explanations with demonstrations. That a student watches you do something doesn't guarantee that he or she "sees" what you're doing. Keep in mind you're teaching answers to folks who don't know the questions.

When explaining something, be sure that you aren't just defining it. I remember a high-school geometry teacher whose explanations made perfect sense but only if you already understood the concepts he was expounding. He defined, but didn't explain.

REINFORCE

When hearing several points about teaching an exercise, people often remember best the last item mentioned. Thus, just before having students show their dogs something, repeat the lesson's most important aspect. For instance, after showing a group how to teach "Sit," I tell everyone:

> Get a few feet away from each other and teach, "Sit." Remember to praise, "Good sit."

Praise is the teaching sequence's vital element. Though I illustrate it while demonstrating how to teach sit, I reinforce the concept by making it the last point students hear just before they work with their dogs.

ENCOURAGE QUESTIONS

Make it easy for students to ask questions. Some folks hold back, often thinking they'll figure it out later. Of course, all that means is they don't understand it now. After covering new material, "Any questions?" and a brief pause, to give students time to think, should be habitual.

EXAM TIME

When possible, "test" students without letting them know testing is taking place. You'll get more accurate responses. Some people react apprehensively when asked to perform. Feeling "on the spot" can hinder their efforts and produce imprecise readings.

TARDINESS

Don't add to a late arrival's embarrassment by calling attention to the fact. Let the latecomer ease into the flow and, if needed, spend a few catch-up minutes with the team while others practice.

FAVORITE BREEDS, FAVORITE DOGS

This trap can ambush any instructor. Have you a favorite breed or breeds? Now, do you often use those breed(s) to demonstrate lessons or techniques? Or a specific dog, one who has become a favorite of yours for whatever reason? I used to, until a friend pointed out my tendency. I saw I was unconsciously snubbing the other animals (and, by extension, their owners) by implication.

Of course, no slight was intended. I was just selecting those dogs easiest for me to read. Still, you can see how this might be off-putting to owners whose dogs you appear not to want to use.

PERSPECTIVE

Encourage students to do their best but don't push perfection. One mark of a good trainer is that he or she knows what to overlook. For example, if while teaching "Lie down" a dog rolls onto his side or back, don't worry about it. To direct a student to admonish the animal, as I've seen done, is to tell a dog who is trying his level best, "Not good enough!" Not only can this send a "Don't try to please" message, it can tell the student that a perfectionist mind-set is reasonable, which it surely is not.

DON'T FORCE A SITUATION

Delay demonstrating force until students can handle the concept. That time may be bare moments into a first class, but wait until you've laid the groundwork. Otherwise, students may misunderstand your intent and perceive you as an abusive power-tripper.

HI THERE!

When taking a student's dog to demonstrate a point, don't just grab the lead and go; start by petting the animal. There's no need to fall all over the dog with tons of warmth, but take the time to say "Hi!" and let the critter know you like her.

Similarly, when returning a dog, don't just hand over the leash and depart. Remain nearby for at least a few seconds. Pet the animal. To some degree you and she have become buddies during the time spent together (at least you should have), however brief, and it's not good to just drop the dog off and disappear.

OUT OF SIGHT, OUT OF MIND

When handling someone's pet, first move the dog well away from the student. Working near the animal's food-giver almost guarantees that the dog will try to keep her attention on her owner.[2]

---

[2]Some folks claim that a dog should be expected to tune out even the distractive influence of the owner, which is why some people spook me more than any dog I've ever met.

More specifically, if you're heeling someone's dog and she sits automatically but in so doing positions herself so she can see her human partner—i.e., incorrectly, relative to you—don't correct the dog. Yes, she's sitting askew, but she's doing so out of habit (keeping an eye on her leader), confusion or insecurity. In any case the mistake is not the dog's. She's just being worked too close to her owner.

WHEN THE OLD TRIED-AND-TRUE FAILS

I've seen instructors lose their cool when their particular method for teaching a given lesson didn't work, when pooch didn't get the word. Often the dog was blamed: "He's not too bright and may not be trainable."

That's callous, embarrassment-driven buck passing. In an extreme case an owner may even consider getting rid of his pet even though the problem was really the instructor. The animal just needed to be shown the lesson via a different technique.

"There is no perfect training method, no single correct or foolproof approach for teaching each and every dog each and every exercise."[3] Not mine, not yours, not anyone's.

If a message isn't getting through, switch gears. Read that animal and find a strategy that will reach him. The answer is there, right at the other end of the leash. Nearly always the dog is trainable, and if you listen the dog will tell you how to make contact.

DO NO HARM

Your opinions may be sought on dog issues. I respond candidly except when doing so would serve no good purpose. For example, I abhor ear cropping. Should someone say, "I'm going to get a Doberman puppy. What do you think about ear cropping?" my answer is unequivocal and direct: "Cosmetic amputation is barbaric and blasphemous." However, should the owner of a cropped dog raise the point, I comment, "Looks like the vet did a nice job," and let it go at that. Candor could only hurt feelings and make the owner defensive.

---

[3] *Dog Logic—Companion Obedience*, 77.

RESPONSIBILITY

Fact: We were under the supervision of teachers and similar authority figures during much of our first two decades. These folks taught us more than the three Rs. We learned that they knew "things"; that their opinions, despite how we felt about them, carried weight; that it was helpful to seek their approval.

True, sometimes all we wanted was a passing grade to shed ourselves of a given class or instructor. Still, we learned to attach meaning to these folk's pronouncements.

Add to those years of subtle conditioning—programming—the common misperception that dog trainers are special types possessing a mystique, and it's easy to see how profoundly an instructor can influence not only student and pet but their relationship as well. Though a practiced trainer may quickly "know" someone's dog more deeply than the student ever will, remember that this "knowing" is the type that's of interest only to professional trainers: breed and gender tendencies, temperament, instinct and drive levels and so on. No one can know that dog like the owner does, in terms of the animal's companionship, affection and role as a member of the family.

Whether you or I see someone's dog as having great potential or very little is immaterial and irrelevant. It not only doesn't matter, it's none of our business. The owner cares a great deal for the animal and that's the end of it. No one has the right to come between owner and ownee, either through judgmental pronouncements or the subtle undercutting effects of raised-eyebrow, disparaging sighs.

I mention this because students sometimes ask, "What do you think of my dog?" Unless the animal is a genetic misfit who constitutes a legitimate threat, find something positive to say about every dog. Am I suggesting you should lie? No. Just do a little looking and you'll find worth in any canine. Anyone who can't do that doesn't belong in the training business, certainly not in the instruction department.

Realize that the student who seeks your "candid, objective, professional opinion" is in reality seeking your approval of the animal. Sure, the love emanating from the dog's eyes toward the owner should be all the answer anyone ever needs, but some folks need a little propping up from time to time. Pooch may not be your idea of much of a dog—he may not even come close—but to the student, that's a very special friend at leash's end, or one that he or she wants to be special. Maybe all that's needed to tip the scale is your smile, "He's a darn nice dog. I think you're both very lucky."

IMPOSSIBLE EXPECTATIONS

Some instructors demand too much. Their standards are so exacting that many students and dogs don't stand a chance of measuring up. Although the pupils and their charges are doing well, if the teacher fails to acknowledge their successes, or cheapens them by accenting the negative through continual nit-picking, students may feel that they or their dogs aren't performing up to snuff. Some may extend that to, "Something's wrong with me and my dog," when in truth the problem is the teacher.

A section of *Dog Logic*'s third chapter is titled, "You're Always On Stage." It says that whenever owners are near their dogs they're teaching the animal, regardless of whether or not they intend to. This also applies to teachers and students. They pick up signals (often without conscious realization) from an instructor's mannerisms, body language and word choice. Their inferences may be inaccurate; and while it may be tempting to rationalize that a student "misunderstood my meaning," a teacher may need to look at, "I need to improve my communication skills."[4]

This is true not just about specific lessons and techniques but about outlook as well. A white-whiskered training adage is that the attitude a person sends along the leash comes back to him or her. That also pertains to communicating with students. If your between-the-lines signals about relating to dogs include patience, love and respect, owners may maintain these values. Likewise, radiating a philosophy of domineering control, enforced subjugation and impersonal harshness validates such a stance as, "the right way to do it." Remember, you're the *teacher*. You're in a position to demonstrate not just the correct way to hold a leash but the proper way to connect with the being that is enhancing your income by receiving your professional attention.

When you train a dog, you affect that one animal. When you teach owners, you affect many, many dogs.

OVERLOAD

A trap similar to the foregoing is teaching more than students want to learn. Few people aspire to become professional trainers, most preferring to make a living

---

[4]An excellent way to evaluate your teaching techniques is to review video/audiotapes of your sessions.

in a less-deranged fashion. Yet beginner classes can be made so complex and cover so many finer points that students can feel overwhelmed and lose interest. I once visited a friend's class during which she gave a brilliant, insightful talk about the nexus between bonding and drive-compulsion concepts. I was fascinated, but most of her students hadn't the slightest idea what she was talking about. My friend was putting out good information but the effort was wasted because the students weren't ready to handle those concepts.

"So I should teach to the lowest common denominator—is that it?" I've been asked that at seminars and though I'm not fond of labels, that one—"lowest common denominator"—has always struck me as most unkind. Sure, each class has an LCD—that's just a matter of statistics—but few of us are qualified to pick out that individual. Simple nervousness can make a person seem less than present at the situation. Besides, to make such a selection would only be to exercise our own biases and prejudices. As William James observed, "Whilst part of what we perceive comes through our senses from the object before us, another part (and it may be the larger part) always comes out of our own mind."

So, no—I'm not saying cheapened classes are any sort of answer. Dumbing down is a childish, repressive if not gutless escape hatch. I'm saying that except in cases of canine mistreatment, including the use of abusive training equipment, we have to limit what we teach to that which people are able to learn when they are ready to learn it.

TO PRESERVE THY SANITY

Consider another *Dog Logic* point: "Accept your pet's best attempts for what they are: his present best. He'll do better with time and encouragement. Fine-tune as you go along." The principle applies to students' efforts, too.

People do their best, especially in group settings. Sometimes that best may not seem very good but the facts remain that it is their present best and it may get better in time. If students goof they simply need more of your help, which—I hope—is why you're both there.

A CAUTION

Be alert for loss of student perspective. Too often some folks see what proper force, leverage and timing can quickly and easily accomplish but, being new to the game, that's all they see. They can lose sight of who is at leash's end. In that context our twofold obligation is to educate the owner and protect the dog.

A PONDERABLE

Question: Have you ever attended a class or seminar permeated by an attitude that the dogs were somewhat peripheral to the event? I have. The focus was so intensely on the instructor, the training techniques, the elbow-rubbing of it all, or all of the above, that the dogs seemed lost in the shuffle.

Core issue: The dog is not superficial to the equation, he's the star. Normal canine potential to give and receive affection, to share companionship, to accept without taking is the stuff of legend. Thus, a thorough Obedience course or seminar, one that offers sound material and respect for *all* participants, owners and pets alike, presents many dimensions: The dog can be a member of the family; it's okay for him to sleep by your bed (or on it); chains are more appropriate for snow tires than for tying pooch; there's no law that says he must be transported stumbling in the pickup truck bed; he *may* ride in the cab. To neglect such concepts is to leave the job undone, while to pay homage to the mechanics of training and to dote on theories is verbal sedation that closes doors and teaches distance. An empathetic, sharing relationship between owner and dog is the summit. Method and style are but minor steps in the journey.

REFLECTION

Good teachers never terrorize their students. To terrorize is to attack, and this results in rejection of what the teacher offers. The result is learning failure.

—HELEN CHUCMAN AND WILLIAM THETFORD,
A COURSE IN MIRACLES

Chapter 6

CANINE AGGRESSION

You're working a student's pet, a good-sized animal. Your concentration is occupied with, say, rectifying a heeling fault. The dog is starting to respond properly, the owner is paying close attention to your technique. You're making mental notes about explaining a concept after you finish what you're doing.

You stop, the dog sits and looks toward you, you reach to pet him. That's when you abruptly sense something in his aspect is different, subtly yet dramatically. Time freezes.

Later you'll tell friends that his eyes had changed, that you felt an accelerating tension in him. As realization hits you the dog explodes, missing your face by inches. You feel the heat of his breath, the brush of his whiskers. His jaws crack together like a rifle shot.

Your eyes record stop-action images, stark in their clarity. Flashing teeth, a spray of saliva, a dreadful intensity rages in the dog's eyes. Adrenaline floods your system as the descriptions "disfigured" and "permanent injury" flit through your consciousness. The animal growls as he wheels for a second rush.

A heartbeat ago the issue was training. Now it's survival. Yours.

And understand: That's the primary goal—keeping that dog off of you. If in the process you can teach him that humans are not meant for biting, so much the better. But that's secondary. Critical is your own preservation.

A heart-fluttering moment.

As you'll see, much of this chapter's format is first-person, singular. The purpose is emphasis. Although this section focuses partly on illustrating how I respond when beset, I don't claim that my ways are right for anyone else. That would be not just impudent but unconscionable: Not knowing your dog-handling skills, I can't advise you specifically about managing canine aggression. My own assets are above-average reflexes, hand-eye coordination, balance, peripheral vision and the subliminal abilities to freeze-frame and react to sequences developing so rapidly as to be a blur to an onlooker. Lacking these gifts I'd often be overmatched as I possess neither great height, weight nor strength. However, for someone with different attributes to try techniques that work for me could be disastrous. My methods might prove not only unadaptable, they could put the handler in greater jeopardy.

Moreover, a guaranteed-to-stop-any-dog formula doesn't exist. If one did, this chapter's theses could be captured in a few lines in another and would begin, "Oh, by the way." Later I relate several personal defenses, but let there be no misunderstanding: In trying something that works for me you could be heightening your own risk. A friend once saw me use a pointed stare and body language to stop cold an attacker rushing toward me. Some weeks later my friend tried the tactic on another dog and nearly got his head handed to him. This animal blew through his mental shield as though it weren't there.

Inventory your physical and psychological assets, considering how each might be valuable during an attack. Take stock of your liabilities, too, and ponder how each might not only hinder you but could actually contribute toward your undoing.

Realize, too, that myriad variables attend any canine confrontation. The first grouping pertains to the dog. His temperament, size, speed, levels of sensitivity to motion, sound and touch, gender tendencies—these are but the tip of this first of three icebergs. The other two represent you and the conditions surrounding the attack itself. Your adeptness in reading dogs, your knowledge of breed tendencies, your physical and mental abilities and dog skills, how you're feeling that day—these only start the list applicable to you. The assault itself, its angle, intensity, target, footing and other environmental factors combine in varying degrees to affect the outcome. Change any one of the foregoing elements, or one or more of many not specifically mentioned, and a new and distinct scenario can unfold.

Thwarting an attack is not an event but a process, one that can develop a millisecond at a time. Opportunity for conscious thought is rare. Analysis comes later. In fact, if a person has to think about what to do, often it's too late.

Mouthing the owner is a bad habit to encourage.

So what does this chapter offer? It describes some canine mannerisms to watch for. It can stimulate thinking before the fact about how you might respond in given circumstances. You may acquire a fuller appreciation of an attack's swiftness, severity and all-out savagery. It can lead you to consider limiting enrollments to certain breeds or dogs of a specific size. It can make you think. My hope is that after reading it you may be better prepared should a dog try to take you out.

Because if you teach classes long enough, one will. The only question is, When?

FIRST THINGS FIRST

Throughout the discussion I postulate that the canine combatant has some size to him. That's characteristic of a dog who can harm a person. Yes, any dog can bite, but I think you'll agree that most trainers would rather take on a rampaging Boston Terrier than an antisocial Giant Schnauzer.

Before handling any dog I inquire whether the animal has a history of belligerence. Sure, that's a commonsense starting point, yet I've seen many an instructor reach for a dog's leash without asking.

I also determine the likelihood of a serious gender conflict between me and pooch. I know a lady whose ex-boyfriend abused her Rhodesian Ridgeback (hence, the "ex" part), such that any man approaching the animal was at risk. That's the type of thing I need to know before taking a leash. It's why I ask during the opening moments of first-week novice classes if any dogs present are biters or otherwise aggressive. My intent is to seek needed information at the onset, and to have witnesses that I asked and to what the responses were.

In approaching any dog, I do so toward the animal's front and from a slight angle to his right. To advance from a dog's left is to take his eyes (i.e., his mind) from the security of his owner. It also can stimulate protective and self-defense drives, since the animal would be between me and his human partner. To approach from the rear is to blindside the dog, a dangerous if not foolish tactic. A head-on strategy is equally hazardous, as the dog may read the approach as openly confrontational.

My movements are unhurried and smooth and my countenance is one of calm as I near a team, speaking first to the dog—"Hey there, pup! How're you doin'?"— and gauging his reaction. I never approach in silence. A no-words advance can seem like stalking.

I'm mindful that of the three postures—lying down, sitting, standing—a dog has the greatest edge in speed and power when sitting. This stance not only aims him upward, he already has his standing balance and his rear legs are angled for an extreme expression of driving force.

While visiting with the owner I seldom take my eyes off the dog. I make brief, gentle eye contact with him but never as a prolonged stare. I keep my balance shifted toward the escape route I've picked should trouble erupt. I seldom offer him my hand—our parents were wrong about that one—but if I do, my thumb is in and my fingers are curled, my goal being retention of said digits. I keep my palm down and my elbow bent, rather than fully extending my arm. This affords me more mobility should a sudden retreat be necessary. If the dog steps forward while being petted, I slide my other hand's thumb or fingers under the animal's collar for control as needed.

A seemingly minor point is my practice of never shaking hands with an owner unless I know his or her pet well. Not only can a dog mistake someone's action of reaching toward his food giver as hostile, I don't ever want my hand in another's grip as a dog fires from the heel position toward my immobilized arm.

Understand: All of the foregoing techniques happen of their own volition. Seldom are any backed by conscious thought. Further, each move is a response to my interpretation of the dog's mental and emotional states.

PORTENTS AND TECHNIQUES

A caution flag goes up should a dog I'm approaching stare at my face. True, the critter may simply be studying my looks, but more likely it indicates a dominant animal with high protective urges.

I'm alert to the dog who ducks behind me during heeling. His action may signify nothing more than curiosity, confusion, insecurity or playfulness, but it can presage darker motives, such as taking me in the leg or coming up my back. My response is not in trying to leash-pop the animal back to heel, as I've seen done. That could not only strain my lower back, it would put my hand too close to a dog who is somewhat in my blind spot. I effect a fast yet smooth about-turn to the left. This keeps pooch within my field of vision while putting him back where he belongs. True, he winds up facing in the wrong direction but that's easily corrected.

I don't use dominant or nervous dogs to demonstrate the "Lie down" lesson. Dominant animals sometimes don't take well to being directed to assume a submissive position, which the "down" position is, especially from a stranger, which I am. Also, a nervous dog can be set off by the close contact that teaching the exercise requires.

*This Rottweiler snapped at his owner. Read this dog's body language and you'll see that the
student's action of grabbing the animal under the jaw has had the desired settling effect.*

When demonstrating the recall with a student's dog, I keep my hands just above the front of my waist, not at my sides, as the animal nears me. Their positioning suggests to a dog who might jump toward me that he shouldn't, and should he try it I have them close enough for a fast push-away.

I'm cautious with any dog who heels wide-eyed and leaning away from me, especially if while doing so he stares at my legs. The animal may be scared and could be targeting me while working up his nerve and bettering his angle of attack.

My experience has been that fearful dogs are not only more prevalent but are more menacing than aggressive ones. Not driven by fear, hostile animals are motivated by confidence. Though they may be recognizable as hotheaded, they are easier for me to manage as I know enough to avoid stimuli that might trigger them.

I don't look away from a dog while working him but neither do I stare at the animal. Not only can some canines interpret prolonged visual scrutiny as threatening, human peripheral vision often better detects sudden movement than does a direct view.

I'm aware that dogs generally telegraph the area they are zeroing-in on; most look where they intend to bite. Also, though not an absolute rule, my experience is that a dog intent on hitting a leg often keeps his head lowered and canted to one side during a rush.

In most instances I hold the leash right-handed. Though I am right-handed, my purpose is only partly dexterous leash control. Given my left hand is nearer the dog, my real purpose is keeping it free as a first line of defense.

I usually keep a forearm between me and the dog I'm working, even when petting (during heeling, however, I keep my left hand above my waist). It serves as a sensory antenna, a barrier when needed, and can reflexively push away an animal leaping toward me. My forearm also can be a powerful deflector in an attack. This is because attackers often go for the nearest limb, and since many altercations that occur take place during heeling. Thus, as the animal goes for my left arm, my right hand, which is stronger and more adept, goes for him. As it was not the hand he'd been watching, pooch seldom even sees it coming. Now I can swat the dog, grab his hair and skin under the jaw (but not the windpipe), quick-wrap the leash around his muzzle or leash-stand him onto his back legs, whichever is appropriate.

Grabbing hair and skin under the jaw is dangerous, but even working a fighter is risky. For me the tricks are in limiting the technique's use to tall, long-haired, loose-skinned dogs, and in keeping my forearms not level or adjacent to either side of the dog's muzzle but well below it and at an upward angle relative to the jaw. Otherwise the animal could turn his head enough to nail my arm. Also, I grab the aggressor just below the point where the neck becomes the lower jaw so that to bite me he'd have to chew through himself.

I recall applying the technique to a pampered Collie who had snapped at his owner and then at me. I grabbed the animal in the manner described above and yanked him against my chest such that we were "beak to beak." Holding him thus I admonished, "Don't you ever even think it!" Many in the class laughed when a second or two later the dog grinned in response. No, he wasn't aggressively baring his teeth; he had submissively flattened his ears, wilted and was giving diplomacy his best shot, a response I later learned he'd developed during puppyhood in reaction to being scolded.

In general, if a student requests help in dealing with pugnacity—"My dog snaps at me sometimes"—I tend to pop the animal's cork so that his hostility occurs at a time and place of my choosing, not his. This not only removes the element of surprise from his arsenal, it allows me to establish a dominant posture that may deter him from bringing push to shove.

But understand this vital point: No instructor is any student's dog's master. That's the owner's ultimate role, not ours. I tell you this because I've seen more than one teacher, when gurgled at, use his or her status to inculcate uncertainty in an inexperienced student, to buffalo him or her into allowing the instructor to pound the dog into submission toward said instructor. The teacher peddled the argument that, "No dog should ever show hostility toward any human." All this, even though the animal had no history whatsoever of aggression.

Such conduct is beyond unprofessional. Rationalizations in defense of them are preposterous. There can be many instances in which canine aggression is not only acceptable but desirable. A dog showing teeth to types who would profess such idiocy as "No dog should ever . . ." bespeaks an insightful canine, one whose counsel should be heeded (which may be why the instructor wanted to shut the animal up in the first place).

FIGHTERS AND FEAR-BITERS

I mentioned in an earlier chapter that I screen students and dogs, denying enrollment to bad-tempered animals. However, as borderline temperaments exist, I sometimes accept marginal dogs. Still, whenever possible I avoid working latent fighters. At the very least I save them for last. By then the group has had time to see that I really do care for dogs, and is more open to accepting what may be a rough confrontation. If I began with a hothead, students might misunderstand my responses, seeing defense of my person as brutality.

I not only try to avoid spooky dogs, I'm wary of those who cling to their owners, hide behind them, salivate or pant excessively or shiver as I approach. This goes double for the creature who not only won't make eye contact with me, but won't even look at me. Any of these signs can indicate a fear-driven animal, one who may arrive at the fight-or-flight stage with very little provocation, real or imagined.

Hence, I let the student do what he or she can, stepping in only if needed. An owner, having fed and cared for the dog, is far less likely to light the animal's fuse. I—a stranger—could precipitate a clash that might not otherwise occur. It may be that the student can handle the critter. Infusing myself into the situation has high potential for:

A) being bitten.

B) injuring the dog.

C) alienating students.

D) all of the above.

Regarding "C," realize that most beginners have never heard the term, *fear biter*. They not only don't know how dangerous such animals can be, if I prematurely leap into a situation students may feel I'm being "mean" to an already frightened dog.

DEFENSES

Throughout the following I posit that I'm working the dog on-leash. Should one lunge at me from his owner's side, I step away and let the student restrain and settle the animal.

My main defense is to hang onto the lead. Experience has taught me that so long as I control the lead I may be able to subdue the animal. Dropping the lead would turn him loose while rendering me more vulnerable.

My response to an upward leap is to spin on one foot, away from the line of attack, as—not before—the animal jumps toward me. To back away would

The author demonstrates why good timing is essential to avoid being bitten.

further attract the dog while heightening his confidence and stimulating his fire. To spin away before the animal commits himself would allow him to redirect at closer range, lessening my reaction time.

As the dog goes past me I yank the lead at a right-angle to his direction of travel or I hip-bump his shoulder, depending on his size, reserving the latter technique for very large dogs. The purpose in either move is to knock the animal off balance. As he lands I jerk him toward my left side. Not only is that the control side, a sideways image presents less of a threat and, more to the point, less of a target.

"OK, what if pooch goes for your legs?"

As the animal commits I yank him upward or sideways, depending on his size (small dogs upward, large ones sideways), while moving the targeted leg out of danger.

Regardless of the angle of attack and my initial response, if the dog persists my next move is to leash-lift him, *not* off the ground but onto his back legs, keeping him there until he settles. In the interim I use the word "No!" a lot.

"That could put a big dog inches from your face."

True, but I've long held that whether an animal misses me by a centimeter or by a country mile, the point is: He missed.

I then lower pooch and command "Sit," to maintain control. Should he continue to altercate, I raise him up again and drive my knee into his brisket, repeatedly if needed. If the animal perseveres I take the wind out of him via a knee to the diaphragm.

As you can see, the process is one of escalating force. It's similar to my philosophy about the use of compulsion in training: "It is not the trainer but the dog who sets the degree of force required. The trainer merely reacts to the dog."[1] Never is my purpose to injure the animal; my objective is to protect myself. While admittedly secondary to preserving good old me, I'm also trying to avoid harming the dog.

Understand, too, that I usually deflect minor-league offensives, such as a raised lip, with a good-natured, "Hey, chill out there, pup." This is because I know that I, as an individual, could not be at the root of hostile behavior by a dog who doesn't know me. Were I to respond paroxysmally, I could trigger a battle in which the animal's psychic survival could become linked, in his mind, with his objectionable behavior. Though ironic, the critter's survival instinct could lead him to sense

---

[1] *Dog Logic—Companion Obedience*, 8.

For me, leaning backward when using a knee to check a jumping dog is safer than leaning forward. Knee checking is not something I enjoy doing, but I find it a preferable alternative to being mauled by a rebellious animal.

that for his identity of self to endure, he must continue the very actions that could one day cause the roof to fall in on him.

However, having said all that, know that with some dogs I'll react to a snarl as though it were an all-out attack. The difference lies in my reading of the animal. With one whom I sense won't fire unless pushed, I deflect. With a dog for whom showing teeth is a precursor, I initiate.

In any case, physical tactics are half the battle plan. The other part is psychological and is of two elements. First, I invade the dog's mind by unsettling his

Body language and calmly spoken words kept this Doberman off of me.

confidence. I do this by virtue of the second part, which is communicating to him my conviction that I can and will emerge not just victorious but unscathed. I send this message via body language, facial expression, eye contact and tone of voice, all of which derive from maintaining an inner calm.

Inner calm is crucial. If I feel it, I may be able to send it; and if I can send it, the dog may adopt it. For my emotions to be part of the event is natural; for them to rule it is to raise the risk of injury, to myself and to pooch. Besides—and this is key—personal anger does not factor into the equation. I'm not mad at the dog—angry people do a bad job of thinking—I'm regretful of the situation and am just trying to contain it. *Canis familiaris* is driven by forces beyond his comprehension. As Johannes Grewe wrote in *The Police Service Dog,* "The dog . . . is unable to understand the reasons for his own actions." When a dog challenges me it's the result of his genetics and/or learning. It's seldom due to the animal's taking a sudden dislike to me personally. While knowing these things wouldn't aid my recovery, they obviate any need for anger and keep me on track. They allow me to see the dog for what he is, and that perception in and of itself can make the difference in a hot situation.

Using the lead in this manner to stand a dog
on her hind legs may keep her off of you.

HOSING, HANGING AND SIMILAR CRIMES

Years ago the practice of swatting an aggressive dog across the muzzle with a length of hose came into fashion. A length of hose may make a good tug-of-war toy but it has no place in canine discipline.

Striking any dog, aggressive or otherwise, with such an object—especially in the "face"—is abuse, nothing less. The action can not only cause head shyness, faulty aim could cost an eye. Also, do it with the wrong dog—or, I should say, the right one—and the animal may see to it that the practitioner winds up nicknamed Lefty!

Also, some teachers can't get through a class without hosing a dog. As mentioned earlier, I've seen instructors push a non–problem dog to the point of feeling threatened. When the animal tried to defend him- or herself—hose time! My thoughts were that the teacher felt a need to display his "power" to the group, and that the inside of his head was in dire need of work.

Another commando tactic that has evolved into common practice is suspending an aggressive dog off the ground by leash and choke collar until the animal changes his ways or passes out. "Mutated" tells the story better than "evolved" as I've seen this so-called technique used for infractions no greater than a slow sit.

To be sure, if an animal has you against the wall you do what you have to do to keep him off of you. But hanging is a last-ditch defensive technique, not a training method. Its only justifiable use is when an instructor or a student is indeed in jeopardy and there's no other way to go. To claim otherwise is to be morally vacant; it is sophistry.

My thought is that extraordinary forms of compulsion have license only in extraordinary circumstances. Should an animal who has the ability attempt to cause me, a student or a dog great harm, all bets are off. I do whatever I have to do to quell the situation. But a broken stay is not an extraordinary circumstance, nor is a crooked sit. Yet I've seen dogs hanged for either transgression.[2]

Besides, being targeted by aggression on four legs seldom necessitates raising the animal off the ground. Hoisting him onto his back legs may keep him off you. In any case, my practice with those rare dogs who are intent on causing grievous harm is to refund the owner's money and suggest he or she consider a more amenable pet. Aphorisms about silk purses and sows' ears aside, a dog who is hostile twenty-four hours a day doesn't match my notion of man's best friend.

---

[2] Other "techniques" I've witnessed have to do with kicking, leash whipping and punishments directed at canine spirit. As this is a book about teaching dog training classes, not animal abuse, I'll spare you the unacceptable details.

TRIGGER

You know that dogs can be aggressive toward humans and can cause a person extreme trauma. Are you also aware how suddenly a canine's sensing of human fear can catapult the dog's responses over the boiling point?

I ask because an emotion any instructor may feel toward a dog is instant trepidation. You start to approach one but a bell dings in the recesses of your mind. The animal's stance, something in his aspect, something in his eyes—they warn you. They say "Don't." And my advice is "Don't."

Don't push the situation. You've recognized something at a subconscious level. Avoidance of that something has kept you intact over the years. Listen to that inner voice. Respect it. If you wish, say "Hi" to the dog, smile (without showing teeth, for obvious reasons) and move on.

Because at least for now the situation is already dangerous. A blink after you felt that internal warning, the dog sensed it. Now he not only has the edge (you're afraid, he's not), he knows it. Worse, his detection of your anxiety can heighten his drive to complete the cycle.

Ignore ego spurts that whisper "But you have to appear in charge!" The reality is first you have to be able to keep appearing. Also, choosing not to confront the wrong dog is surely an in-charge decision.[3]

Given the business you're in, you deal with many dogs. It's just a matter of statistics that some may try to "wind your clock." In that context, fear of those animals is both healthy and rational.

Recognize also the wisdom in the adage, "Scared money never wins." Dealing from fear can lead a person to make bad decisions or bad moves.

Now, how often does such a "Whoa!" situation occur? Hardly ever. So why have I spent over 300 words on the subject? Because dogs come armed, to the teeth (if you'll forgive that), and in terms of caution, better you should learn from these pages than from an emergency-room visit.

I WON'T WORK WITH A . . .

In the preceding chapter I asked if you have a favorite breed or breeds. Now I'll ask, Are there any breeds that make you uneasy? Breeds that, for whatever rea-

---

[3] I know an instructor who later said he "knew better but went ahead anyway." Born with ten fingers, today he has nine.

son, you'd rather not handle? There are two that unsettle me that way—never mind which ones—and my manner of resolving the issue is to question extensively callers who own such dogs, especially about matters of temperament and history, and if I have any doubts about the animals' psychological soundness or the owners' candor, I enroll them not.

"But you train and teach for a living. How can you refuse to work with ___?"

Real easy. I intend to keep making a living.

REFLECTION

Here's a lesson for you: Never insult seven men when all you're packing is a six-gun.

—Colonel Sherman Potter (Harry Morgan)
in the "M*A*S*H" T.V. series, 1985

Part III

COMPANION
OBEDIENCE

Chapter 7

OVERVIEW

Please examine the following basic-class summary.

TRAINING OUTLINE—COMPANION OBEDIENCE

EXERCISE	WEEK 1	WEEK 2	WEEK 3	WEEK 4	WEEK 5
Sit	On command	XXXX	XXXX	XXXX	XXXX
Heel and Auto-Sit	On-Lead	Mild Distracts	Heightened Distracts	As Needed	Hand Signal
Sit-Stay	6 Feet/ 1 Minute	15 Feet/ 2 Minutes	30 Feet/ 3 Minutes, Signal	Handler Out of Sight/ 1 Minute	Handler Out of Sight/ 2 Minutes

continues

TRAINING OUTLINE—COMPANION OBEDIENCE *(continued)*

EXERCISE	WEEK 1	WEEK 2	WEEK 3	WEEK 4	WEEK 5
Down-Stay	XXXX	15 Feet/ 2 Minutes	30 Feet/ 3 Minutes; Signal	Handler Out of Sight/ 1 Minute	Handler Out of Sight/ 3 Minutes
Over Jump at Heel	XXXX	XXXX	At Heel/ Low Height	As Needed	As Needed
Recall	XXXX	XXXX	6 Feet	15 Feet	30 Feet/ Hand Signal
Finish	XXXX	XXXX	XXXX	Teach	With Recall; Hand Signal
Stand-Stay	XXXX	XXXX	XXXX	XXXX	20 Seconds

ANALYSIS: COURSE CONTENT

The commanded sit and its cousin the sit-stay are useful to keep a dog stationary for brief periods. One application would be when company appears at the door—a sitting dog not only can't get underfoot, she can't jump on anyone.

Heeling allows an owner to move pooch from point "A" to point "B" with little or no effort. The related automatic sit at heel keeps the animal under control when movement stops. This allows an owner to visit with someone encountered during a walk without the dog becoming a nuisance.

As the down-stay is more comfortable than the sit-stay, "Lie down" is practical for keeping an animal stationary for extended periods, such as when visitors drop by or during family meals.

"Over jump at heel" is useful for negotiating fallen branches, puddles and the like. The activity is also foundational for teaching one's pet to jump into and from a vehicle, and for competition jumping.

The value of the recall ("Come to me!") is self-evident.

The finish is optional. I include it for pet owners who want to go that extra mile. The exercise's purpose, of course, is heightened bonding, control, and increased canine understanding of the heel position.

The stand-stay, in addition to being good mental discipline, is functional for grooming.

Hand signals for stay, heeling, come to me and the finish are electives. They're offered to allow owners to enter more deeply the dog's world of communication, which is largely effected by body language.

A course's effectiveness is rooted not just in subject matter but in the order in which concepts are presented. While not every lesson builds on a previous one, many do, specifically and generally. A specific example regards teaching a dog to come when called: It's easier if the dog already knows "Stay." In that case, control is transferred from the stay element to the recall command. An example of the general sense of lesson building concerns "Lie down." Some dogs resist the command but the contention rate is lower among those who have learned via preceding heel-and-sit training that, "You must!"

ANALYSIS: LESSON SEQUENCE

FIRST WEEK

"Sit" is the initial class's first command. This starting point is not arbitrary; several reasons underlie beginning with this lesson.

First and second, sit is the easiest element for most beginners to teach and for most novice dogs to learn. Third, given my training method, the exercise swiftly opens the dog's eyes to the reality that the owner is in charge, effortlessly so. Fourth, the quick success that most students achieve in teaching "Sit" raises their confidence that they can and will be able to train their pets. Fifth, as sit is a static exercise, it quickly makes the class environment safer by providing needed control of dogs who arrived barely under control. Sixth, it has the side effect of showing students that it's not only easy but alright to make their pets obey. Last, it teaches a component needed for the next lesson: Heel on-lead's automatic sit.

Why get into heeling next? For that matter, why add any other work at this point? Why not just call it good for now with the "Sit" exercise?

Answering in reverse order, "Sit" is not enough to cover at a first class. Most students can teach more and, of equal relevance, most dogs can learn more. That, and part of my teaching-training philosophy is that once you're on a roll, stay with it. Besides, if "Sit" were the day's only lesson, the ensuing week's practice sessions would give heightened meaning to the word *boring*. Also, it would make for a very brief first class.

By advancing to heeling soon after teaching "Sit," the teaching process is kept alive and many dogs begin to see that their people are in charge and trying to communicate with them. Were the first class limited to "Sit," those points might be less apparent.

The automatic sit is included in teaching on-lead heeling so as not to send pooch a fallacious message. I've seen classes where the auto-sit was added—commonly via untoward force—after a week of heeling that ended each time with the dog being told "Sit." Then, on day eight, the command was replaced with a correction. Such after-the-fact altering of a pattern constitutes changing the rules of a former lesson, an unfair if not abusive tactic.

The sit-stay is the day's final lesson. It is last in the sequence as most dogs are amenable to resting after a few minutes of exercise via moving at heel. Also, by following a motion exercise with one that forestalls movement, the contrast allows most dogs a better chance of discerning that a new lesson is being taught. A sitting dog, when first shown "Stay," can become confused about what she should do. "Sit" means do this, "Heel" means do that—both call for action on the dog's part—but "Stay" means do nothing. You and I can handle the conceptual distinction between "Sit" and "Stay," but a dog, being positively oriented, can become perplexed when first shown a negatively-based command, especially since being told "Stay" is adjunct to doing something she's already doing.

SECOND WEEK

During this class we add the lie-down command. Like the sit, the purpose is stationary control. Unlike the sit-stay, the down-stay's purpose is to keep a dog in one place for long periods.

I've been asked, "Since you teach sit and stay as distinct lessons, why don't you teach down and stay separately?" The answer to this is in two parts. First, "Stay" is "Stay." Whether sitting, lying down or standing, "Stay" means "Don't move." Hence, the stay element of the down-stay is not new material. Second, when most pet owners want a dog to lie down, they intend for her to stay put for a time; thus my practice of linking the two concepts at the onset.

The second class consists of a single lesson, as contrasted with three during the initial meeting, to give the teams additional time to become more proficient at heeling. Also, there are easier things to teach a dog than "Lie down." By making that exercise the sole new work for the second week, students and dogs are better able to focus on the exercise, undistracted by other new requirements. True, the time and distance factors of the stays increase during week two, but that seldom causes problems, as the change is gradual, subtle and in any case does not constitute a new and distinct lesson.

THIRD WEEK

"Over jump at heel," aside from its practical applications, is part of my curriculum simply because most dogs love to jump. It's fun. The previous two weeks' heeling lessons have shown the dog that she must respond to the command to heel. Given owner unfamiliarity with animation techniques, which most beginners aren't ready to learn at this stage, some dogs heel unenthusiastically. Over jump at heel can improve attitudes by showing them that heeling really can be enjoyable.

Also, there's a subtle sound-alike link that can accent enjoyment of another of this week's lessons, the recall. "Hup" is the over jump at heel command. The recall command is, "Here." The dog learns that the "H" sound in "Hup" means fun. By teaching over jump at heel before teaching the recall, often the "H" sound links the happy attitude to the recall.[1]

The recall could be taught during the second week, i.e., before teaching "Lie down." However, when taught the recall before being shown "Lie down," some dogs confuse the two commands. More than once I've seen an animal come when told to down, especially when commanded at a great distance.

This potential for confusion increases when the commands are "Come" and "Down." They can sound much alike to a dog, especially a novice. Competition trainers can get away with using both because they're dealing with unchanging performance patterns; but on the street, so to speak, it can be very different.

---

[1] "Dogs can think that fast? To react to the beginning sound of a one-syllable word?" As the person who asked me those questions was an avid AKC Obedience competitor, I asked if he'd ever seen a dog initiate a recall in response to the sound of her name, without waiting for the command itself, even though the name and command were vocalized as one. "Now that you mention it . . . ." the man nodded.

Another reason for delaying the recall until week three is that I teach it through drive; and the first two classes are based in compulsion, to show dogs who generally are accustomed to having their own way, "You must obey!" By introducing the recall after the dogs have had a couple of weeks of being shown that they must respond to command, resistance to the recall lesson is virtually nonexistent.

Also, since a key to teaching the recall is that the dog enjoy the work, it is scheduled for the third class to capitalize on the bonding that the preceding training has already enhanced. Last, placing the recall after teaching stays can contribute to instilling a positive recall attitude. Stays are seldom exciting, and because the recall releases pooch from a stay, the dog may further see the exercise as attractive.

The stay signal is taught during the third week to heighten canine concentration. It is delayed until this class because most dogs' attention spans before this time are inadequate for teaching the signal.

FOURTH WEEK

As stated earlier, the finish is optional. I tell students that if they'd rather have pooch recall directly to heel, that's up to them. But I also point out that an advantage of teaching the finish is that it reinforces the heeling command's true meaning, that it pertains to a position relative to the handler.[2]

Teaching the finish is delayed until the fourth week because canine focus is essential to learning the exercise. Other lessons have heightened this concentration enough that the dog is now more likely to respond to a known command given in an altered setting—the dog facing the handler, rather than being at his or her side.

Out-of-sight stays are initiated now because, as the training to date has enhanced the animal's confidence in her human partner, a dog is less likely to be anxious when her handler disappears. Also, the effect of stays successfully having been practiced in ever-increasing time-and-distance settings makes it more probable that the animal will hold her position when first realizing that her owner is leaving her sight.

---

[2] I use the same command for heeling and the finish.

FIFTH WEEK

The stand-stay is delayed until the final week because, in terms of concentration, it is the hardest stay to maintain. A dog must move much of her body to break a sit- or down-stay, but to violate a stand-stay she need only move a paw.

Hand signals for heeling, the recall and the finish are offered as electives to heighten canine attention on the owner.

OTHER "TRAINING"

Throughout the program everyone is encouraged to play with pooch daily, using a tennis ball, Frisbee or whatever seems to turn the animal on.

You need to work with your dog for about fifteen minutes a day on what we cover at class. You also must be willing to play with her for at least that long. Give no commands during playtime and keep the two activities separate for now. Later, you may merge them, but not yet. At this stage a dog needs times that she knows are just for fun.

REFLECTION

Learning is not attained by chance; it must be sought for with ardor and attended to with diligence.

—ABIGAIL ADAMS

Chapter 8

Just Before a First-Week Class

GETTING READY

Before the first arrival, affix enrollment forms and pens to several clipboards. Using a table for sign-ups may seem practical but can be risky as it brings dogs into close proximity with one another. Since untrained canines are not likely to "keep their cool" around unfamiliar animals, a dogfight can easily erupt under the above circumstances. Clipboard usage allows students to complete paperwork at safe distances from each other. It also shortens enrollment time as clipboards can be circulated, so no one has to wait for an opening at a sign-up area. Not incidentally, a clipboard can be an effective shield against an aggressive dog's sudden rush toward you.

Inspect the training site for leavings that might stimulate class dogs to contribute. Also check for debris that could be injurious or distractive, cleaning up or removing as needed.

Then spend a few minutes doing whatever you do to relax. Perform a little mental hyperventilating. Center yourself. A phrase from the days of my youth is, "Get your head together." Teaching can be draining; make sure your tank is full. Release anxiety, shelve concerns, clear your mind.

91

GOALS

Once you've stilled yourself, fix in your mind the objectives for this first class. Beyond the obvious, I mean. Sure, you're going to show students how to teach certain Obedience functions, but you have other aims that you won't state.

First among these is to help owners relax. New students are often jittery, and regardless of how much phone time you've spent with them, many will have no idea what to expect in an actual class situation. Some will feel that everyone knows what's going on except themselves. Others will think, "My dog is the worst of the lot." Maintain an open, positive, chipper if not lighthearted persona, making every attempt to put folks at ease. Coming on with a cold, impersonal, all-business attitude only reinforces student anxiety. Until people are at least somewhat collected they'll have difficulty learning—tension causes defensiveness, and defensive students tend to resist rather than absorb.

Second, much of what you'll be doing throughout the series is showing people that it's okay to make their dogs behave. You will be teaching by doing, demonstrating that it's alright to curtail canine mischief. At the same time, make it clear that no one has to be tougher than the animal and the situation call for.

Last, you're going to touch on three concepts. One: training must occur at the dog's level of understanding if pooch is to learn. Two and three: how dogs being pack animals affects the human-canine relationship, and that the owner's goal must be to become pack leader. Make people see that the pack instinct is a powerful motivating force, one the dogs couldn't abandon even if they wanted to.

You must remember, the dog is the one who turns around in place several times before lying down, because nature tells him to flatten grass and look for snakes and other hazards—even when he's sacking out in your living room!

Nodding heads and comments like "I've seen my dog do that" are commonplace in class at that point.

Do you see where he lives, people? You see what you've got there at leash's end? Training won't change that. It won't take that aspect, and others like them, out of the dog. Training will allow you to communicate with your pet, and—being a dog—once those lines of communication are established, he'll respond. Become your dog's leader—not a dictator, now—and you'll discover a greater friend and partner than you ever thought you'd be blessed with.

GIVE YOUR BEST FRIEND A FEW DAYS OFF

Leave your dog(s) at home during the first few sessions. Bringing a trained animal to initial classes can be a study in boredom for him and can distract you and your students from the job at hand. Also, should you have to deal with an aggressive animal (and hostilities, if they are going to occur, are more probable at a first or second class than during subsequent ones), your dog might attempt to protect you by joining the fray. This might be an understandable reaction on your dog's part but it would worsen a bad situation for all concerned.

Also, prematurely bringing your beautifully trained dog to class and showing what he can do can easily inhibit beginning students. Contrary to your intentions at motivation, running your pet through his routines—even just a prolonged stay—can lead some enrollees to feel they'll never be able to train their dogs to a similar degree. Of course, while this remains to be seen, this attitude can lead to dropping out before any serious progress can be reasonably expected.

Though it's not necessary that you bring your dog to any meetings, the optimum time to do so is the fourth session. Students far more appreciate a trained animal after working with their own dogs for a few weeks.

"I see that, but what about when I want to demonstrate an exercise's finished product?"

Use a student's pet. You're adept at reading dogs so you should be able to spot a quick learner. As novice exercises can be quickly taught in their entirety, after briefly working a bright animal, the lesson should have taken. Thus, you should be able to successfully demonstrate the current goal.

Or let one of your students do it. I've yet to teach a class that didn't have at least one all-star team, one that caught on quickly. After showing students a given action and letting them try it for a few minutes, call the group together and ask whoever is doing best to demonstrate.

A third approach acknowledges that it's rare that at least one former student isn't present doing brush-up work. Ask that person to perform the exercise. Let him or her and pooch be in the spotlight awhile. This acknowledges your former student's efforts and demonstrates that your training methods work.

LIKEWISE . . .

Just as it's unwise to bring a trained dog to a first class, it can be equally defeating to make your dog's only appearance at the last session. Many students will compare their graduation-day results with yours and may decide that they've not done well. This, notwithstanding that your pet doubtless has many, many training hours under his belt, uh, collar.

HERE THEY COME!

Make life easier—and safer—for everyone by seeing that each dog is securely leashed before entering the training area. Watch for frayed leashes and collars that are so loose that a dog could slip free.

Consider having a few extra leads and collars available for loan if not for sale. True, you've described on the phone the type of equipment that students need but that doesn't guarantee they heard you.

Though it may seem helpful for you and your sign-up assistants to offer to hold leashes while each new arrival completes the paperwork, I suggest you don't. Should a dogfight erupt you need your hands free. The time it takes to return a dog to an owner might make all the difference.

As each student finishes enrollment, advise him or her to walk pooch around the training site and allow the animal to sniff and explore the area (but not other dogs). If trees are part of the setting, direct students to keep their male pets away from them lest the verticality principle come into play.

"KEEP THEM APART!"

Remind everyone that no dog is to contact another. Greenhorns sometimes ask, "If the dogs can't sniff each other, how will they ever become friends?" While the unspoken answer is that Obedience training is the goal, not dog-to-dog friendship, explain the three very good reasons for prohibiting sniffing.

First, sniffing or any direct physical contact can transmit disease. Second, an Obedience goal is to teach a dog to key on the owner, not on other dogs. Letting animals contact each other could undermine that message. Finally, as between people, bad chemistry can exist between dogs. All it takes is one "wrong" animal meeting another and we can have a potentially serious dogfight on our hands in a heartbeat.

Of course, should a fracas occur, you might have to be the one to break it up. Not only would that put you at risk, it could cast a negative aura over the new class. That I've yet to have a novice-class fight is due to my insistence that each dog arrive on-leash and that there be no dog-to-dog sniffing.

Occasionally you'll run onto a well-meaning yet misguided soul who isn't satisfied with your "Sniff ye not!" policy. "But I want my dog to meet all the other dogs."

Such comments indicate the person may perceive his or her pet as akin to a furry human. It smacks of parental concern at a first day of school. You must show the individual that introductions are more appropriate for people, and that in any case you don't allow sniffing. There's no need to be abusive or dictatorial, but when a novice is unknowingly placing him- or herself or pooch on dangerous ground, clarify your rules and be prepared to enforce them with a mix of diplomacy and necessary firmness.

DANGEROUS MISMATCHES

Though more likely to occur when teaching children, be watchful for clearly overmatched students. We've all seen it a few times: a hesitant, mild-tempered human trying vainly to handle a large, powerful, dominant, exuberant dog. No, the animal isn't "bad," but he may be an accident waiting for a place to happen. Understand, I'm referencing extreme situations, ones where—if such a dog were to lunge at another—the owner would be powerless to hold him back. That's not just unfair to other students and dogs, it can put you at physical and legal risk.

My practice is to take the leash (with which the owner is usually relieved to part) and advise that what's needed is more authority on the owner's part. If no one in the individual's family is better able to train the animal, I meet privately with the student for the first class or two. By then the dog should be under sufficient control to be safe around other animals.

ON YOUR MARK, GET SET . . .

Unless all scheduled students have arrived, wait a few minutes past the announced starting time before beginning the class. Late arrivals are disruptive, especially at a first-week session.

REFLECTION

Perhaps the most valuable result of all education is the ability to make yourself do the thing you have to do when it ought to be done, whether you like it or not; it is the first lesson that ought to be learned; and however early a man's training begins, it is probably the last lesson that he learns thoroughly.

—THOMAS HUXLEY

Chapter 9

FIRST WEEK

It's just minutes before a first-week novice class is due to start. The last student is signing up, dogs are barking, some are growling, owners are waiting for things to get underway, restraining their pets, and some wide-eyed souls appear to be wondering what they've gotten themselves into.

If you're new to the business—or, at times, even if you aren't—you may be having the same thought. It all seemed so easy when you were a student. Today, as an instructor, things are a little different. Everyone's paid their fee, and now, as the minute hand nears the appointed hour, you have to earn it.

To do that requires you earn something else; two "something elses," in fact: confidence and respect. You earn your students' confidence by demonstrating that you know what you're talking about, and their respect by showing that you understand how it can feel to be a beginner. Neither can be demanded, they can only be earned.

Chapters 9 through 13 present a succession of word "film clips" excerpted from my basic-obedience class series. The montage portrays my instructional attitude; my way of communicating lessons and concepts to people who, for the most part, have never trained a dog. My intent is to take you through a series as an observer, to depict reality rather than just tell you about it.

Dogs do the darndest things at a first-week class.

GO!

Everyone, let's get started. Form a big circle. Keep a safe distance between dogs. Don't let them sniff each other—that can cause a dogfight. You'll know if a fight starts: I'll be up the nearest tree, shouting advice and encouragement.

As handlers position themselves, canine behaviors vary from curious to withdrawn, playful to apprehensive. These are all within perfectly normal ranges.

If an animal is overly sportive I direct the people/dog teams nearest her to move away, creating more room. If need be, I sufficiently quiet the critter so that I can proceed without further interruption, keeping her with me for the moment if necessary.

My manner is relaxed and informal. Similar to, "What you send down a leash comes back to you," a rigid, top-sergeant demeanor can project nervousness to students. They, in turn, may transmit anxiety to their pets. Some earnest training is about to commence, yes, but that doesn't mean an instructor must take him- or herself overly seriously.

I talk to the group as a whole while slowly moving from team to team, saying "Hi" to each student and petting each dog.

Let them settle, people. Let them calm a bit. Some of these animals are seeing more dogs today than they ever knew existed.

Keep your dog near you. Pet her. Kneel or sit next to her if you care to. Give pooch a few minutes to get used to this setting, to whatever she thinks is going on.

I move to the center of the circle and ask everyone to take a step or two toward me. This shrinks the circle's area, making hearing easier and bettering the group's psychological cohesion.

"WELCOME TO DOG TRAINING 101!"

That's how I "officially" open first-week meetings. The phrase informally solicits attention while putting students at ease. It also sets the tone: True, the moment is at hand, but that doesn't call for suspending compassion or humor.

KICKOFF

The first topic is how to hold a leash securely, to prevent a dog from pulling it from an owner's grasp. While the lesson is important for its own sake, it allows students to learn something quickly, easily, and to do it successfully. I demonstrate while I describe.

That loop at the end of your leash—put your thumb through it. Use whichever hand feels "right." Now close your hand over the loop. Hold the excess with your fingers or with your other hand. This grip makes it harder for pooch to pull the lead from your grasp.

While correct leash grip is reflexive to you and me, for beginners, whose total knowledge thus far is how to find your teaching site, this is an important moment, one that can prompt "How about that!" comments. The students just learned something. They just entered the world of dog training.

WHATZAT?

To sustain student involvement I point toward a well-known breed, signal the owner to remain silent and ask the group, "What's that?" Occasionally some wit offers, "It's a dog," and that's okay as the response affords everyone a chuckle.

"Very good! But what *breed* of dog do we have here?"

We go around the entire class this way, one animal at a time, until each has been identified. By then the people are starting to relax, they're participating and most important, they're listening.

"WHAT IS OBEDIENCE?"

That's my next query. "That's why we're here: Obedience training. What is it?" Essentially, the answer I'm seeking is: Teaching a dog to respond to commands such that she does what she's been taught regardless of whether or not she feels like it.

It's one thing to teach a dog what a command means. It's another to show her that commands aren't open to a vote. Obedience isn't a democracy, you know. We can show pooch any number of times what a command calls for, but training doesn't occur until we also say, "And by the way, dog, you have to do it."

"SMELLING-SALTS, ANYONE?"

"People, this here is a pinch collar."

Some subjects are best approached bluntly; pinch-collar usage is one such topic. Holding a medium-link pincher high enough so it can be seen easily and I announce, "Many of you will need one of these to train your dog."

This is an attention-grabbing, welcome-to-the-real-world moment, one that can arouse "My Gawd!" reactions, and cause some students to look at me as though

I'd just popped through a hole in the dimension. Doubtless you've seen and perhaps have used pinchers. But to someone new to Obedience, the device can be perceived as nothing less than an instrument of torture. Nothing could be further from the truth, of course, but how do you communicate that to folks whose main concern is, justly, their pet's welfare?

My solution: Hit the issue head-on.

God-awful appearing thing, isn't it? No argument, it looks fearsome. But let me tell you something: This is a classic case of what-you-see-is-not-what-you-get. No, it won't poke holes in your dog. The links' ends are dulled.

This gadget's purpose is to simulate the sensation of mom's teeth on the neck of an animal who instinctively recognizes the feeling. Ever seen mom discipline one of her puppies? She grabs the little one's neck with her teeth and the pup calms. Not only is this collar kinder than a choker, if it could injure your pet I'd be the first one to tell you not to use it. Let me show you something.

Most classes include at least one large, exuberant canine powerhouse. That's the dog I start with. Often she's barely controllable and her actions can cause chuckles: "Let's see how far our teacher gets with this character!" As I approach the team I address the owner in a voice all can hear.

Tell you what: It's pretty obvious you've got a lot of dog there. Let me show you how this collar can make life easier for both of you. If you want me to take it off after a few minutes, I will. Fair enough?

I can't tell you what to do if someone turns you down—I've never had it happen. I like to think that's a tribute to my winning charm (?) but I suspect that, in truth, owners of such dogs were desperate enough to try anything.

I attach a pincher and snap the leash onto the collar. I move the dog away from the group and slacken the lead. The animal steps away from me, intending to investigate something that's caught her eye. The leash tightens, the collar contracts, the dog turns toward me. I effortlessly guide her around the training area. Now students are faced with a seeing-is-believing situation.[1] I return to the group, momentarily keeping pooch with me.

---

[1] Today I won't let a dog "hit" leash's end. That would be too much pressure on an animal who, at this point, could have no notion of what's expected of her. I pay out only enough slack that the dog feels collar pressure within two steps of leaving me. Should a dog bound away, I lessen shock by instantly taking up slack and redirecting her from a right angle, which requires less force, of course.

See? This collar is power steering, and I didn't hear a dog screaming her head off. In fact, I didn't hear the animal make a sound. Did you?

By now owners are seeing that a pinch collar isn't unkind after all, that one might be useful in their training programs. It's not uncommon to hear, "Put one on my dog, will you?"

People, let me tell you something about training and dogs: You have to operate at your pet's level of comprehension. She's the one being trained so your lessons must be understandable to her.

Our best friend here is a pack animal. What you call a family she calls a pack. For you to train your dog you must become pack leader in her eyes, Alpha, number one. That's who a dog instinctively respects and follows. As a pinch collar simulates the sensation of mom's teeth, its usage is a quick way to enter your dog's world. It's that simple.

I return the dog to her partner and go from dog to dog, attaching pinchers on those whom I read need one.[2]

FLASHBACK

Consider what just took place, beyond the obvious, that is. Sure, the group was shown that pinch collars are humane and useful. They were exposed to the concepts that training must occur at a canine level of understanding and that dogs are pack animals who follow a pack leader. But beyond that, why did I start with what seemed to be trouble on four legs? Why not begin with a milder temperament, or at least a smaller dog?

First, the animal I picked was rowdy, not aggressive. More often than not, rowdies are searching for direction; they're seeking a leader (hence, their frantic boisterousness). As I momentarily fulfill that need, it's easier to start with a Type-A than with a laid-back counterpart.

A side benefit: Owners are seldom aware of that looking-for-a-leader aspect about exuberant dogs, so what they see is a seemingly out-of-control animal being quickly and easily brought into line. The effect is to raise their confidence about what they may achieve with their own pets.

---

[2]For dogs on whom a pincher would be excessive, I suggest a flat leather or cloth collar. In rare instances when a choker is proper, be sure to demonstrate how it should be correctly worn.

Why not start with a wee dog? Because smaller members of the canine persuasion can be pound-for-pound as tough as any on the planet. Were I to start with a tiny animal and find her neck was like bull hide and her disposition said "Make me!" I'd risk alienating the group by responding appropriately.

SIT

Next I demonstrate how to teach "Sit," the first of today's lessons. It's all very well to register an initial class without dogs present and to lay out the framework for the next several weeks. But my experience is that the average person not only doesn't care to spend any more time than necessary in teaching basic obedience, he wants to show his pet things today—now. Besides, a pretraining meeting might not only formalize the informal, it would extend the series by a week, and there's no need for a Companion-Obedience class to last longer than five weeks.

In choosing a "Sit" candidate I prefer a Labrador-sized or bigger breed; it's easier for most novices to see what's happening when watching a larger dog. While I've been talking to the group, I've been looking more at the animals than the people, to spot trouble before it starts and to get a reading as to which dogs may present what problems. In picking a dog for this first lesson I'm searching for one who's attentive, relaxed and interested in the proceedings. She's easy to spot: She seems to be studying me and doesn't flinch from a few seconds of eye contact. Once I've chosen a dog, I ask to borrow her and take the leash.

I walk backward toward the center of the circle, keeping my attention on the dog while patting my leg and saying, "C'mon, pup," to attract her. The walking-backward technique is to draw the dog along without using force: Most dogs will follow a person who is walking backward. Were I to turn my back I'd risk blocking the animal emotionally, causing her to resist going with me. Also, should I mistakenly have chosen a "wrong" dog, I'd chance being bitten by taking my eyes off her. Besides, I'll be telling the students repeatedly during the next few weeks to keep their focus on their dogs, so I exemplify the point right from the start.

While allowing the animal a moment to sniff and otherwise check me out, I tell the class that I'm going to begin the dog's education by teaching her to sit on command. Then I do just that.[3] By the fourth demonstration most dogs respond properly. As soon as this one does, I pet and tell her what a superb job she's doing.

---

[3]Training techniques referenced in chapters 9 through 13 appear in *Dog Logic—Companion Obedience*.

Temporarily keeping the animal with me, I pose a question I'll ask many times during the series: "What did you see?" I'm trying to involve the students and cause them to think. First-week responses are generally few and far between because students don't know what to look for. So if the group's collective answer is a blank stare, I recount my "Sit" training method step by step.

Then I return the dog to her owner, borrow another pooch and show her "Sit," so students can visually correlate what they just heard. Then, while petting the dog:

Now, did being made to mind make either dog resentful? Did the procedure hurt them in any way? I think not. Look how this one's wagging her tail. Notice her expression as she looks at me. I don't see displeasure, I see a happy dog, one who's enjoying trying to please.

I move the dog a few steps, have her sit again, and repeat the process until she gets the idea and sits without help.

Beautiful! That last sit was on her own. She did it without any coaching from me.

While praising the dog I notice some grins and nodding heads. The students saw the animal respond, too.

Give it a try. You'll be surprised how quickly your pet will get the idea. Move a few feet away from each other and teach "Sit." Remember the praise: "Good sit."

For the next several minutes I watch the teams, noting who is having trouble with what. If a serious problem is developing I help that pair sort things out. With difficulties that are merely symptomatic of first-time trainers with untrained dogs, I reflect that I once lived there too and call no attention to any problems just then.

I withhold overall comments until the class is back together, then direct observations to the group, not to individuals. It's unprofessional to single out a person and list his or her shortcomings. If I later see that someone is still experiencing untoward difficulties, I have a word with him or her away from the others.

After a few minutes I call everyone together.

A FREQUENT TENDENCY

People, you're doing really well. I don't see any unusual problems but some of you are making one common error: repeating "Sit." Tell your dog once. Otherwise you're teaching him to ignore you. If you give a command only to repeat it, the dog either couldn't hear you, doesn't understand or has just expressed his opinion about what he's been told to do. Show him from day one that he must respond quickly to your word.

Questions? OK, work on "Sit" a bit more. Then we'll get into heeling.

HEELING AND AUTOMATIC SIT

After borrowing a dog, I command "Sit" and position myself such that he's in the heel position.

Heeling finds the dog maintaining the heel position, at your left side, close but not touching.

Someone may ask why the dog is at the left.

Most people are right-handed. With pooch on the left, your strong hand is free for things like unlocking a door, carrying a package or maybe just shaking hands with someone.

If you'd rather your dog heel at your right, that's OK but if you ever compete in Obedience the dog must be on the left; and changing the heel side on one who's learned a location can be the devil's own work.

Heeling also requires the dog sit automatically—that is, without a spoken "Sit"— whenever you stop. The idea is to maintain control when you're standing still, so you can visit with someone without the dog wrapping the lead around the person's legs, ascertaining gender and generally being a nuisance.

Let me show you how to teach heeling.

I tell the dog, "C'mon, pup," move away from the group and introduce the animal to heeling.[4] When we return to the circle I ask, "What did you see?" If answers are in short supply, I outline my techniques. Then I keep perspective on track.

Any dog's heeling can get only so good in a few minutes. For a dog to heel she has to be constantly aware of where you're going. These animals aren't used to concentrating like that, which is why—for now—I'm taking only a few steps between stops. By stopping often I'm also accenting the auto-sit, which most of these dogs can learn before class today ends. I'm showing the dog heeling, yes, but the quick result I'm after is the automatic sit.

I heel a few steps to keep the dog on a roll and to allow students time for absorption.

---

[4]Readers of *Dog Logic—Companion Obedience* know I precede heeling instruction with *Leash Taming*. In classes I avoid this extra step, incorporating it into initial heeling lessons.

My heeling command is "Fuss." Like "loose" with an "F." It's German for "foot." You command "Fuss" every time you start walking. I don't use "Heel" because when we teach "Come to me" the command is "Here," and "Heel" and "Here" sound alike, which can confuse a dog.

I "Fuss" the dog a few more steps.

Very important: The leash stays slack. Walking with a dog on a constantly tight lead is not heeling, it's guiding, or dragging. It causes constant collar pressure even though the dog is responding properly. That's wrong, clearly. The idea is that the animal should remain at your side as though there were no leash. That's heeling.

Questions?

One that's often asked (which I raise if a student doesn't) is, "When do I praise my dog for good heeling?"

As she takes her first step with you, or as she works at staying with you on a turn. That's when she's most aware of doing something, as compared to when she's just trotting in a straight line. Tell her "Good Fuss" but keep moving; don't stop to praise.

OK, work on heeling for a few minutes. Remember, just a few steps between stops.

I watch the teams, helping where needed. After several minutes I call the group together.

Take five, people. Stand or sit next to your dog. If she wants to stretch out for a bit, let her. Just so she stays near you and doesn't try to go to another animal. Pet your dog while we cover a few things. Make that a habit during these breaks.

Question: How many dogs are already auto-sitting?

Several hands go up.

Okay, once your dog gets the auto-sit idea, continue to praise "Good sit" but drop the "Sit" command. Otherwise the message is you'll always tell her to sit, which you won't.

I pause to let that sink in.

Let's say your dog's been sitting automatically—she's got the idea—then one time she doesn't sit; she stops and just stands there. What do you do?

Answer: Leash pressure. Start with a gentle pull. If all that gets you is a glare, tug harder. If the dog still resists, yank the leash; jerk her into a sit. Then heel a couple of steps and stop to see if she got the word.

It's called a correction—a sit correction, in this case—and it's used to give a dog a choice. She can mind or be made to mind. It's up to her.

Questions?

"How hard do I yank?"

That depends on how tough your dog is. I expect the Border Collie over there would require very little force, while that Rottweiler might take a good deal.

But carve this in stone: Start gentle. Don't risk scaring the dog. Pinch collars don't need a lot of force to be effective, so take it easy. Remember, you can always get tougher.

Something about correction to keep in mind: It's not anger on your part. It's merely a mechanical response to a dog's refusal to obey a known command. It's for when you give a command, the dog says "Nope" and you say "You must!"

Questions?

SIT-STAY

We've one topic left to cover: the sit-stay. I've saved it for last because it's the easiest. Heel your dogs a step or two, then get them sitting.

After borrowing someone's dog I demonstrate how to teach the sit-stay, when to praise and how to correct for movement.

Try a quick sit-stay of a couple of feet, so I can see you've got the idea.

After a few seconds I tell the students to return and praise their dogs.

BEFORE THEY DEPART

I end each class by reviewing the highlights of what was covered, pointing out the goals for the upcoming week and asking for questions. Don't be concerned if your closing, "Questions, comments, wise and witty sayings?" is met with silence: Many students still won't know enough about training to formulate questions.

Then I distribute written material: *Novice Obedience and Training Hints*. I also furnish a sheet titled, "Week 1," which lists the current week's objectives. These items are discussed in chapter 5, "Teaching Guidelines."

One last bit of business. I want to be sure that you know how to attach and remove the pinch collar. This one I'm holding is the medium-link size, but what I'll show you applies to all sizes.

After the collar demonstration:

Remember this about collars: Don't ever leave any collar on an unattended dog. With the wrong collar, like a choker, she could catch it on something and strangle herself to death.

I let a few seconds tick by.

A final word has to do with attendance: Be here! You may feel a bit overwhelmed by all that's gone on today—the first class is always the hardest—but stick with it. Next week it gets easier.

"Really?" someone may ask.

Even during classes in "formal canine obedience," humor should be part of the scene, for dogs and people alike.

True story. By the end of the third class you'll be wondering what all the fuss was about. So hang in there. Besides, if you don't show up we'll talk about you.

That last part isn't true, of course, but it gets a laugh and does wonders for attendance.

Okay, that's it for today. Give me a call if you have any problems. From what I've seen today, I think you folks are going to do fine—better than you might suspect, in fact. Thanks for coming. See you next week!

IT WON'T TAKE LONG

A few days after the first session, call each student and see how their dog's training is going. You'll head off problems and your thoughtfulness will be appreciated.

Make it clear you're not singling anyone out. Some people can worry that you're calling because you think their dog is a problem. Comment, "I call everybody after a first class, just to see how the training is going."

REFLECTION

Dogs begin in jest and end in earnest.

—H. G. BOHN

Chapter 10

SECOND WEEK

People, form a circle, please, like you did last week. Get your dogs sitting at heel. OK, how'd the week go? How are you and pooch doing?

Answers vary from "Pretty good" to a cataloging of woes, often the former. We deal with reported problems before today's practice and new lessons get under way.

During this opening segment I move around the circle, checking collars for proper attachment and leashes for wear.[1]

DISTRACTIONS—HEELING

Tell you what: You see these four posts I've placed around the training area, creating the corners of a large square? Line up between them, along the four sides. Keep plenty of room between yourself and the next team.

Once everyone is in position, I continue.

What you're going to do is heel as a group around this rectangle. The idea is to simulate taking pooch for a walk with other animals nearby. I'll be telling you "Go" and "Stop." On "Go," command "Fuss" and get moving. On "Stop," stop naturally. Don't slam on the brakes.

---

[1] Habitually eyeball collars and leashes. Along with finding pinch collars attached by only one of the two prongs per link, I've seen frayed leashes that were a hairbreadth from snapping.

If the team ahead of you is slow, go around it. Don't bunch up. If your dog shoots ahead, immediately do an about turn; go the other way. Just be sure you know what's behind you. Don't run into another team.

Questions? No? We're starting in this direction—Go!

Barring major problems I let the class heel once around the rectangle before the first "Stop," so students can get their rhythms going. When I do stop the group I wait a few seconds before starting it again, to let the people collect themselves and praise their pets. Then I start them again and, after they've gone about halfway around, stop them and talk about tight leads, slow sits, owner inattentiveness and erratic praise. There are often plenty of each.

You're looking good, people. You've obviously practiced this week. But I'm seeing some common tendencies that will work against you if we don't fix them now.

One is tight leashes. Put some slack in your lead. It doesn't have to be much, just enough so your dog can't feel where you are and must work at staying with you.

Second, keep your eyes on your dog. You don't want to walk while staring at your pet for the rest of your days, but for now keep track of what he's doing.

Slow sits—some of you are stopping and then waiting several seconds to see if your dog will sit. Listen, when you stop, if pooch isn't sitting within a second, correct him. Show him he must sit quickly.

Last, where's the praise? These dogs should be hearing "Good fuss" and "Good sit" a lot. There will come a day when you won't praise for everything they do but that time isn't now. It's way too soon to pull away from constant approval.

So what do we have? Slacken your leashes, keep your eyes on your dog, watch for slow sits, and praise—don't forget the praise.

Questions? No? Alright, we're still heeling in this direction—go!

After the students heel once around the rectangle I stop and start them again. If anyone is still having trouble with tight-leash heeling or slow sits, usually because of a quick dog and/or an owner's slow reactions, I work the animal and show the student how to anticipate the dog's actions. I also mention that an attribute of correction is that it's not just a matter of "How hard?" but "How quick?"

Now, please consider the following.

> [No] one should give a dog more than he can handle. Anyone can lose a novice animal on a sudden turn but . . . [that] isn't the idea. Challenge a dog according to his level of understanding and ability—that's the idea! Make heeling just difficult enough so that he has to work at it.[2]

---

[2] *Dog Logic—Companion Obedience*, 125.

My approach to teaching classes entails a similar note. As each dog has vary-ing potential, every group produces different chemistries. With many classes, second-week start-stop heeling in a square is as much as they can handle. Con-versely, some groups create a confluence of learning eagerness that can boggle the mind. Each student seems to spark every other. When I run into a bunch like that I push the envelope.

Go. [Ten paces later] *Turn around; go the other way.* [Ten paces later] *OK, run. Not flat-out but at a jog.* [Ten paces later] *Now your normal pace.* [Ten paces later] *Stop. Praise "Good sit." Now leave the dogs—they're sitting, so just say "Stay" and go to the end of your leash.* [Pause 30 seconds] *Back to your dogs. Tell them "Good stay."* [Five-second pause] *OK, we're heeling in this direction. Go.* [After ten paces] *Stop.* [Five-second pause] *Go.* [After ten paces] *Turn around—go the other way.* [After five paces] *Do it again; turn about.* [After five paces] *Stop. Sit-stay to the end of your lead.* [While students are at leash's end:] *During a stay, move around. Do things. Tie a shoe, visit with someone, but keep one eye on your pet at all times. The idea is for pooch to build the habit of keeping his attention on you during stays, which moving about can teach, if for no other reason than to see what you're up to.* [After sixty seconds] *OK, back to your dogs. Tell them "Good stay."* [Five-second pause] *Heeling is in this direc-tion. Go.* [After one time around the square:] *Stop.*

Circle up and take five. Relax. Tell these dogs how well they're doing. Pet them a bunch.

I allow everyone a few private moments with their dogs and to visit with their neighbors, if they wish. Then I talk about the nature of practice.

A tad tiring, isn't it? This one-thing-to-another bit, I mean. Sure, but let me tell you something. Practice like this—brisk heeling with speed changes and turns, switching from one activity to another—can accomplish more in five minutes than can twenty minutes of slower work. The dog has to maintain concentration on you to keep up, and that starts building the habit of staying in tune with numero uno.

Questions?

After dealing with any queries—and motivated groups often have several—we continue.

DISTRACTIONS—STAYS

Let me show you something about stays. Heel your pets a step or two, then get them sitting. Now command "Stay" and go to the end of your leash. OK, when I tell you, return to your dogs, stand next to them but don't say a word to them. After a few seconds, leave again, but without any command. Don't leave in a heelinglike manner. Just drift away. Your dog should stay. If she moves, don't forcibly correct—she's likely confused—but show her that just because you came near doesn't cancel your "Stay" command. Otherwise, you won't be able to get near your dog during a stay without her moving.

Training a dog to hold a stay while petting another student's dog is an excellent control exercise.

Questions? OK, go back to your dogs, then leave again.

After a few seconds I tell everyone to return and praise their pets.

Then I outline another distraction.

Try this. Command "Stay" and go pet a nearby dog. Hang onto your leash and keep one eye on your own dog at all times. If you'd rather not pet one of these dogs—if one of them spooks you—just pet someone else's. Go ahead. Watch your own dog.

After the students return, I stress that the idea is still one of distraction work, that it doesn't matter what an owner does after leaving, the dog should maintain her position in any case.

There are all kinds of petting.

RELEASE CUE

Someone may ask, "How do I release my dog from a stay?"

Heel him out of it.

"OK, how do I release my dog from heeling?"

What you're asking is how do you release your dog from working, from command, yes?

"Un-huh."

There's a training concept known as a "release cue." It tells a dog that he's on his own for now. I don't recommend the notion, for the simple reason that I don't ever want to say

*to my dog that there are times when he and I aren't us. To me, the pack is always on sim-
mer. I "release" my dog by petting him, telling him what a great dog he is, slipping his
collar off and going about my business. If pooch wants to tag along, that's fine. If he'd
rather do something else, sort of go his own way for a time, that's OK, too.*

*Work ends but obedience doesn't. We never officially stop, like we never officially be-
gin. We just always are. That way, like the relationship, the animal's obedience is always
on, bonding is always on.*

*Now, if I haven't talked you out of using a release cue, for heaven's sake
don't use the commonly heard, "OK." That word is too ingrained in our vocabularies to be
effective. Use "Later," or something else you prefer, but not, "OK." OK?*

APPLICATIONS

*Last week some of you asked about problem behaviors. The difficulty mentioned most often
was jumping on people. I said we'd be better off waiting until your dogs knew some things
before we got into these issues. You now have a tool for stopping pooch from jumping on
folks. What is it?*

Silence.

*OK, someone appears at your door, you invite the person in, and here comes pupper at
full leap. Isn't that about how it goes?*

Nods and chuckles.

You can stop the problem with two words. What are those words?

Blank stares.

People, how can a sitting dog jump on anyone?

A few "Ah's" as realization dawns.

*Sure, saying "Sit" and "Stay" to a dog who is reliable with these commands solves the
problem. A sitting dog can't jump on anyone. That's part of why I asked you to pet each
other's dogs during a sit-stay a few minutes ago: to get the animals used to the notion of
being petted by a stranger while maintaining a sit-stay.*

"What if my dog isn't wearing his collar when someone comes by?"

*Good question. Answer: Arrange for a friend to be in cahoots with you, to come by,
knock on the door, and wait for as long as it takes for you to get the idea into pooch's head
that he can either respond to "Sit" or you can put the collar and leash on him very fast and
make him sit, that you will ignore whoever's at the door until he minds. True, you can't
neglect legitimate callers, but your dog doesn't know that. Get the idea?*

Most folks comprehend the strategy without further explanation.

Here's another application, especially for people who live in an urban location. When taking your dog for a walk, always stop before stepping off a curb. The stop makes your dog auto-sit and that enhances control before stepping into a street. Your pet will learn that a curb calls for a sit.

Questions? No? OK, next we're going to cover teaching your dog to lie down, and at the next class I'll ask you for applications of the command. Be thinking about it. You see, teaching pooch several lessons is dandy, but the real value is in how you can use them.

DOWN-STAY

Last week we covered three lessons. Today we cover one: Lie down. We don't give up on last week's material. We just add "Lie down" to the list.

For now, though, practice this new work separately. During the week, practice heeling and sit-stays, take a break like we're doing now, then work on the down-stay. Separating lessons can accent the new material, which makes learning easier. After three or four days, integrate the down-stay with the other work.

Today marks the last of your German commands. From here on it's English. The word you're going to use is "Platz." That's "Platz," with a "P." It rhymes with "lots" and means "place," as in "Place yourself on the ground." We use Platz because by the time most dogs get to an Obedience class, "Down," the conventional command, already has meaning. It usually means get off something or someone and often the dog has learned to ignore it. Rather than fight through all that, it's just easier to use a new word.

Let me show you how to teach "Platz."

I walk someone's pet a short distance from the group and show the animal what is expected by the "Platz" command. After three or four repetitions I return to the students and ask, "What did you see?" By now people are beginning to tune in on what to look for, and it's not unusual for a student to enumerate the teaching steps.

I move the dog a few steps and down him again, to let the students see the procedure once more while the teaching method is fresh in their minds.

Once pooch was on the ground I moved him after a few seconds and repeated the exercise. I didn't leave him there for several minutes. Otherwise too much time would pass between demonstrations for easy learning, for accenting the action of lying down.

I again move the dog, command "Platz," and this time he downs without help. After praising the animal I return him to his owner.

Teaching "Platz" can have its amusing moments.

In a few minutes you'll show your dog "Platz." I showed the animal what I wanted by pushing downward with my left hand on his shoulders while holding his leash with the other, so he couldn't take off.

Also, I used "suggestive force"—the barest of tugs on the leash. Curiosity often leads a dog down but if not, I would have swept his front legs forward with my right hand.

The "right" way to get your dog on the ground is the one that works for you. You just need to experiment a bit.

I pause for a few seconds to let things filter in.

I didn't push the dog straight down. He could resist by bracing his front legs. So I took him to one side. Notice which way, if any, your dog is leaning. Take him down in that direction. That may cause him to down somewhat crooked, but remember the first objective is to get him onto the ground.

One last point: If pooch rolls onto his back or side don't worry about it. Tell him "Good Platz" and be thankful he's not contesting you tooth and nail. Dogs who roll over are usually showing submission and that's OK. Most will mature out of the tendency faster than it can be trained out.

Alright, unless something isn't clear, you guys try it. Get some distance between each other and teach "Platz." Sing out if you need help.

I observe the group's efforts for several minutes, helping out as needed, and then call the students together. After outlining my style of Platz correction, and cautioning that its use is proper only after the dog clearly understands the command, I offer a suggestion.

Now, let me make life easier for you in terms of teaching "Platz." Today we started with heeling and stays. Then we moved on to "Platz." We showed some pretty tired dogs a command to lie down when it looked pretty good to them. See?

Likewise, if it's a nice day, heel in the sunshine and "Platz" in the shade. Again, this can make the idea of lying down more attractive to your pet.

Questions?

I circulate a roster of student's names, dog's names and breeds compiled from the enrollment forms. I ask the students to verify spelling as diplomas will be prepared from the list. Then I distribute the Week 2 sheets.

There's something you all should know: Next week it gets even easier. You'll see. Give me a call if you have any problems. Thanks for coming.

REFLECTION

An old dog will learn no new tricks.

—THOMAS D'URFEY

Chapter 11

THIRD WEEK

People, circle up, please. How are you and your dogs doing? Any problems we need to hear about?

We discuss training difficulties, if any, that have occurred during the week.

Okay, let's try something. Tell your dogs—just once, now—"Platz."

The animals' responses vary from quick compliance to "nobody home."

Alright, you guys whose dogs hit the ground, take five. Just pet your dogs for a bit. Everyone else, command "Platz" once more and if the animal doesn't respond, either step on the leash or yank it downward, depending on your pet's sensitivity.

The students do as instructed.

Now move your dogs a few steps, get them sitting and command "Platz" again. Be ready to use force if needed.

Generally each dog goes to ground but if one or two are still resisting, I have those students repeat the process until each animal complies.

NO COMPRENDO

Throughout the series, be watchful for dogs who, for whatever reason, haven't figured out a command's meaning. With "Platz" the problem is often that the animal has learned that the command means he will be placed on the ground, that he doesn't need to do anything, perhaps even that he shouldn't. As must be obvious, correcting a confused dog is totally out of line.

Should the problem occur, don't chastise the owner. You have to assume that the person has done his or her best. That best may not be as good as you think it should be but remember that best is relative: Pretty lousy for one person can still be best for someone else. Just work with the dog until the difficulty is straightened out, then let the owner take over.

MORE DISTRACTIONS

Last week you heeled in groups around a rectangle. In terms of being obedient around distractions—nearby moving animals, in that case—your dogs did darn well for having had just a week's training.

Now, how could we turn up the heat on that type of conditioning? How could we make it more challenging? Fair, but harder?

Often someone offers the notion of dogs heeling past each other, which is what I have in mind. If no one does zero in on the concept, I introduce it.

Let's have half the group, from the Boxer to the Collie, over here. Form a line with teams spaced about eight feet apart. The rest of you bring your dogs over here, about thirty feet away, and line up opposite and facing the first group.

I position myself between the two rows of dog/handler teams.

Okay, the question was how to make heeling near other dogs more difficult. You're looking at the answer. What's going to happen is that when I tell you "Go," both groups are going to heel their dogs to where the team opposite them is standing. Obviously, you're going to pass one another in the process.

Memorable, as-the-dawn-broke comments I've heard over the years are:

"Lord have mercy!"

"I just remembered I have to make a phone call."

"My hospitalization isn't paid up."

"Not without a whip and a chair!"

Now, a little common sense here, folks. We're simulating a heavy pedestrian-traffic situation. So do what you'd do in such a setting. That is, don't heel your dog right at another. Give each other some room, as you would in public.

One rule: Watch and control your own dog! Every one of you is counting on each other to do that. Your pet can glance at another as they pass—that's normal behavior—but if your dog takes so much as one step toward another, don't wait to see what's going to happen next. Yank him toward you and keep moving.

All set? Okay, then. On your mark, get set—wait a minute! Let me get out of the way—okay, go! Watch and control your own dog!

I've used this distraction pattern for more years than I care to remember and it's never led to a dogfight. Yes, I've seen some animals consider the notion, but I've seen them corrected sufficiently so that they learned they'd best listen to their handlers. A trick to running the exercise safely is that just before it starts, give the students but one thing to remember: No dog is to reach another.[1]

You made it! See, that wasn't so bad. Both you and your pets did really well. Praise those dogs. Let them know how impressed you are.

I let a few seconds tick by.

Now, stay alert—we're going to do it again. No dog went for another but I saw a couple of them think about it. By now they may have worked up enough nerve, so keep your eyes open.

Okay, ready? Go! Watch your dog!

This time there may be an indignant squawk from one or more dogs as they're corrected for trying to visit another animal.

Not bad, people. Not bad at all. One more time. Go! Watch your dog!

After this third pass-by exercise I give everyone a minute or so to relax.

Anyone here who's surprised how well pooch is doing?

Someone usually is. "My dog's doing great!"

Sure is. They all are. What this means, of course, is that you guys are doing a good job of training.

---

[1] Position any dog with an iffy temperament at the end of a line.

Okay, one more time. Ready? Go! Watch your dog!

Just as the two lines near each other I stop the group.

Stop. Sit-stay—leave your dogs. Hang on to your leash and keep an eye on your pet.

After thirty seconds I have the people return to their dogs and complete the heeling pattern.

Okay, let's add another dimension. This time, a couple of steps after you pass the person coming toward you, turn round and go back the way you came. Go! Watch your dog!

Once the teams have returned to their starting positions I start them again.

Okay, straight through this time; no turn. Go! Watch your dog!

As the two lines near each other I stop them and integrate last week's lesson.

Stop. Tell your dog "Platz!" Okay, command "Stay" and leave. Hang on to your leash!

After a minute or so I have the students return to their dogs.

Circle up, people. Let's take five. These dogs are doing well. So are you. Any questions?

After a brief respite I touch on a common problem.

There are a couple of things you need to watch. Some of you are commanding "Fuss" and jerking your leash just before or as you give the command. And sometimes when a dog doesn't sit I'm seeing the owner yank the leash simultaneous with saying "Sit." These aren't just incorrect procedures, they're unfair.

Say "Fuss" and give pooch a chance to respond; don't jerk the lead reflexively. Otherwise your dog has no chance to respond and may quit trying.

With the auto-sit, don't command "Sit" in the first place. We're no longer telling these dogs to sit; it should be automatic. If there's no sit, correct the animal.

Listen, don't worry if you've been doing either of these things. They're very common with beginning trainers. Just realize the problem and quit doing it.

APPLICATIONS

Last week I told you that this week I'd ask for uses you've found for having your dog hold a down-stay. What'd you come up with?

"It's sure handy when the family is having dinner. My dog used to be such a pest then," is one often-heard comment. "I have my dog do it when I'm on the phone," is another. "Sure makes driving the car easier with the dog lying down," is a third. I could mention several more and I imagine you could add others to the list. The point for instructors is that it's important that students find uses for obedience. Otherwise their motivation for continued training can evaporate.

OVER JUMP AT HEEL

At this point I borrow someone's dog. In making my selection I'm looking for a friendly, outgoing candidate and—most important—the taller the better. You'll see why.

You see that eight-inch board I've set on its narrow side? I'm going to teach the Scottish Deerhound here to jump over it while heeling. The functional reason for teaching jumping is to make it easier to get a dog in and out of a vehicle, or over an obstacle during a walk. In addition, I teach this exercise to put some fun into heeling—most dogs love to jump. Watch what happens.

I heel the dog toward and over the board, commanding "Hup" as I jump over the hurdle. By the third or fourth pass the animal is jumping the object. After returning the dog to her owner I ask the group a question.

Okay, why did the dog jump? I mean, she could have just stepped over the board. That's the main reason I picked her: She clearly doesn't need to jump. So why did she?

"Because you said 'Hup.'"

That's part of it, sure—the dog sensed I was trying to tell her something. But "Hup" has no built-in meaning for a dog. No word does. What else was going on?

"Well, you jumped over the board yourself."

That's right, and . . . ?

"The dog imitated you!"

Exactly! Had I just stepped over the board, the animal would have done the same thing. Dogs are tremendous imitators.

You see, that's why your attitude toward your pet and his training is so important. Essentially, your dog will imitate it. Perhaps you've heard the adage, "If you think you can, or if you think you can't, you're right."[2] Likewise, when you radiate confidence in your pet, he may adopt that attitude toward obedience. A trainer who sends a message of doubt, however, creates hesitancy in his or her dog.

I pause and pet a dog or two, to allow time for this last comment to sink in.

We're making a subtle shift in training technique here, too. So far we've been showing pooch that he must accede to commands; that the alternative is being forced. Now we're entering a form of training that accents the fun of it all.

Now, if anyone here—human or canine—cannot safely hop over that board, anyone with knee, ankle, back or similar problems, don't try it. The same goes for folks who think their pets might get underfoot and cause a fall. Otherwise, what I want you guys to do is heel your dogs over the board one at a time. Create a big circle that intersects the jump. Build up a little speed as you approach the board, command "Hup" as you jump over it, and head for the end of the line. As the dog lands, keep moving and praise, "Good hup." If a dog balks, encourage him over. If an animal simply won't go over the board, lift him over. After jumping your dog, heel to the end of the line and get ready to jump again.

One important element before we start: Put a safe distance between each other so no dog is thinking about another too close behind him, or about going for one in front of him. Speed and jumping can excite—a dog might think that you're speeding up to pursue the animal ahead of you—and we don't need a dogfight. Be ready to leash your dog back should trouble develop.

Questions? Okay, then, go ahead. Remember to praise "Good hup!"

Within minutes I'm hearing students laughing and watching them having fun with their pets. It's at times like these that I'm reminded how much I enjoy teaching Obedience classes. After the circle of students has used the jump three or four times, I call the group together.

---

[2]This aphorism is generally credited to Henry Ford, Sr.

Do you remember my telling you last week that, "Next week it gets even easier"? Now you see what I was talking about. This "Over Jump at Heel" is pretty easy training, yes? The dogs are starting to see how much fun obedience can be, too. I saw a lot of wagging tails out there. Let me show you some equally simple training.

HAND SIGNAL: STAY

Get your dogs sitting, if they aren't already. Just heel them forward a step and stop. They'll sit.

Okay, leave your pet on a sit-stay but without using sound. Just hold your palm in front of your dog's beak and step away.

No dog moves. After ten seconds I tell the owners to return and to praise silently via petting.

Why didn't any dog move? You didn't say "Stay." Why did they stay put?

"We've been using the hand signal all along. They're used to it."

Right! And the result bespeaks a truth about dogs: They key on signals—body language—more than on sounds. Sure, sounds are used in the wild, but signals—which are silent and therefore safer to use—are the main form of communication.

Signal training can enhance bonding, too. Anyone know why?

Novice students seldom get this one, understandably.

Signals are more intimate; the rest of the world does not get to hear. Also, as signals are by nature more in keeping with canine communication, you're operating closer to your pet's level of relating.

Now, if pooch misses your signal by looking away just as you give it, and as a consequence moves when you leave, correct him. Don't go overboard with force but let the animal know that he should keep his eyes on you during training. You see, that's another reason for teaching this signal: to teach your pet to be more attentive to you.

Now let's get on to today's primary lesson—"Come to me." It's easy too.

RECALL

After borrowing someone's dog, I move the animal away from the students, telling them, "Watch what happens." Then I teach the animal to come to me. After running through the training sequence three or four times, I return the dog to his owner and ask the group my usual question, "What did you see?" Students report their observations and soon a clear picture of recall training emerges. Two points that students may miss, however, relate to the leash and to the sit element.

Teaching the recall. Note that the Malamute has begun moving in response to his handler, not a tight leash.

Did you notice that the leash never tightened? I want my dog to be happy to come to me. Pressure could dampen that attitude. What did I do as the dog arrived?

"You said 'Sit.'"

Right. Why? Why do I want the animal to sit?

Beginners seldom sense this.

I commanded "Sit" to keep pooch with me. Otherwise, what does a dog do when you call her? If she comes at all, she either runs past you or circles you a time or two and takes off again. "Here" is to call pooch to you; "Sit" is to keep her there. You want your dog thinking about the sit she's going to do when she arrives, not considering whether she will come to you. If you take it as a given that she'll come to you, putting your focus on the sit, your dog will imitate that attitude and come to you reliably.

I pause to allow processing.

Now, as your pet catches on, drop the spoken "Sit." The dog's response will become automatic, like the auto-sit at heel. Also, as she gets the idea, fade out the moving-backward technique. Okay so far? Questions?

I pause a few seconds.

Now, three quick points. One, don't correct the animal if the sit isn't perfect. You don't call a dog to you and then pressure her. That just isn't done, not if you want her to ever come to you again. Clumsy the critter into a sit if you must but don't correct her.

Two, don't bend forward when calling your dog. Stand normally. Bending forward can slow a dog's advance or even stop her.

Three, know what is behind you! I don't want you guys running into each other. That's easier than you might think when you're concentrating on events in front of you.

Okay, move well away from each other. Teach "Here." Praise "Good here" as pooch comes to you, "Good sit" as she sits.

After a few minutes I call the group together, distribute the Week 3 sheets and ask for questions.

See you next week, folks. You're doing well, really well. So are your dogs. Thanks for coming.

REFLECTION

No symphony orchestra ever played music like a two-year-old girl laughing with a puppy.

—BERN WILLIAMS

Chapter 12

FOURTH WEEK

Okay, let's get going. Any problems we need to talk about? Any questions?

After dealing with whatever issues students raise, we spend a few minutes examining a facet of how dogs "think."

Let me show you something. First, have your dogs lie down; tell them, "Platz."

Once the animals are in position, I continue.

Here's what I want you to do. In a minute, when I tell you, command "Sit." Say "Sit" just once, and—most important—don't correct your pet if he doesn't sit. One time only now, tell your dog "Sit." Then hush.

Seldom does a dog sit.

Okay, why didn't the dogs sit? A sudden collective case of canine brain fade? Heck, "Sit" was the first command they learned; and since then they've been shown automatic sit at heel, sit-stay and to sit after coming to you. Why didn't any of the dogs sit?

Silence normally ensues.

Well, let me give you a clue in the form of another question: Do dogs perceive sitting as an action or a body position? How do they see that sort of thing?

More silence.

Let's put it to a vote: How many for an action?

A few hands tentatively go up.

Alright, how many for a position?

Some more hands are raised.

How many for, "Beats the hell out of me!"?

Many hands are up now and amid chuckles someone may see the light.

"Well, my dog does what I tell him now; he's no longer resisting. So since he'd do it if he could, he must not be able to see how. So he must see sit as an action. If he saw it as a position, he'd just do it."

That's pretty good dog-think. To a dog, "Sit" means, "Put your butt on the ground," and he can't do that when it's already there. "Sit" doesn't mean, "Push yourself up with your front paws," which is what he'd have to do to sit from the down position. These dogs may be wondering if by telling them "Sit," you guys have taken leave of your senses.

You see, dogs don't generalize certain forms of learning. You expected them to sit because in this type of setting, humans tend to think in terms of a finished product, in this case a sitting dog. But a dog thinks more in terms of, "How do I do this?"

Now, what good is this lesson to you? Just this: If someday you teach your pet something and the training falls apart—it doesn't seem to be getting through—I'll bet you skipped a necessary step in the teaching sequence. You left out something connecting what the animal knows with what you want him to do. If your dog seems to be resisting a new lesson, before you get on him consider that he may not have been shown what you want him to do in terms he understands. Set yourself down and rethink.

Questions?

Next we move on to distraction work started two weeks ago.

During week two you heeled around a rectangle, to accustom your pets to heeling near other dogs. Last week you heeled toward and past each other, and did stays and Platzes near each other. This week it gets better.

Heel away from one another—get some distance between you—then pick out someone, heel toward that person, stop, introduce yourself and visit for a few minutes. Shake hands if you feel like it. Maybe pet the other person's dog. Then move on to someone else.

That is, you're meeting someone on the street and your dog should sit and remain at your side.

But people, this is not a social encounter; it just looks that way. It's a training session. Teach your dog that just because your attention appears distracted from him doesn't mean his obedience is suspended.

Know at all times what your dog is doing. Keep an eye on him. And don't say, "Sit" if your pet doesn't sit when you stop. Correct him into position.

Use your dog's name when you meet someone. That's what you'd do in the real world, as the person probably would ask your dog's name. Hearing his name may make your pet want to move forward, toward the individual, but you should make sure pooch remains sitting.

Questions?

A common query is whether an owner may command "Stay" when meeting someone, to keep the dog at heel.

You can, but better the dog should learn that he's expected to stay at your side, that that's part of the heeling and auto-sit requirement. Dogs learn behavior patterns, and I teach my dog that the pattern is that he must stay next to me unless I say otherwise.

Other questions?

If there are none I continue.

Now, if any of these dogs makes you uncomfortable, just don't visit with that team; or, at least, don't pet that particular dog.

Alright, have at it. Visit with one another for a time. Remember: Watch your dog!

After ten or so minutes I call the students together and spotlight their progress.

People, if you're wondering how you and your dogs are doing, let me ask you something: How would you like to have tried this "meet your neighbor" bit at the first class?

This question tends to drive home the point that a great deal is being accomplished by everyone, the dogs included.

Alright, let's work on recalls. For a few minutes, get away from one another and practice calling your dog.

After a brief time I call the students together and outline recall training for the upcoming week.

The next step in teaching "Come to me" is to lengthen the calling distance to fifteen feet. Make the increase gradual and either acquire a longer leash or tie some cord to your present one to maintain control.

OUT-OF-SIGHT STAYS

The most useful stay is when you leave pooch's sight. Commanding "Stay" and walking a few feet away to turn and stare at your pet is useful at an Obedience class, but the stay you really need allows you to disappear. I'm going to borrow a dog and heel her over near that outbuilding. You guys watch what happens.

Then I acquaint the dog with the concept of out-of-sight stays. After returning the animal to his owner, I visit with the group about what just took place.

Okay, I know you saw me leave the dog on a sit-stay and step around the corner of the building, thereby leaving her sight, but what else did you notice?

"You didn't let go of the leash."

Right! Anything else?

Comments are rare at this juncture.

First, when I left the dog's sight, she had no idea how far away I actually went. For all she knew I left town. To a dog, once you've left her vision you are as gone as anything can be. That's just how dogs "see" things.

But to make it harder for her to figure out that I was just around the corner, I positioned myself so that when I was away I wouldn't throw a shadow that she might notice. When working outdoors, I also make sure the wind is from a direction that won't carry my scent to her.

I pause for a few seconds.

Another thing: When you practice these stays at home, do yourself a favor and enlist the aid of a helper. Have a nearby person who appears to be doing one thing, like hammering on a fence, but who is in reality watching your dog. If your friend coughs or drops a hat—whatever signals you work out—you respond by reappearing and reinforcing that pooch is not to move once you've said "Stay."

Now, use different helpers and different signals. I've seen the following happen more than once. Handler and dog have been working on out-of-sight stays for several days. Same helper each time and the broken-stay signal has been a cough. Then, one time after the handler commands his sitting dog "Stay" and departs, the animal lies down. The helper coughs but the dog hops back into the sitting position before the handler can return.

I pause to facilitate comprehension.

Sure, the critter had learned that the cough meant the handler was coming back. They're dumb animals, yes, in that they can't verbalize. But stupid? Not even a little bit.

Okay, try this out-of-sight stay business so I can see you've got the idea.

FINISH

This next is optional. You call your dog to you and he arrives and sits in front of and facing you, right? Now we want to show him he is to return to the heel position. The move is called the finish. Let me show you what it looks like.

I use one of my dogs to demonstrate the exercise, or if a former student is visiting the class, I ask him or her to show the group the finish. A memorable comment by an equally memorable student of years ago typifies the novice reaction: "Lord, God A'mighty!"[1]

---

[1] Do you remember the first time you saw the move? I recall mine. It knocked my nine-year-old eyes out.

See how it works? The dog is called, "Here." After he arrives and sits facing the handler, the animal is told, "Fuss," and the critter returns to heel. He goes from the "here" position to the Fuss position.

Now, what good is it? The finish, I mean. If you're not training for competition—you have to do the finish in competition—why bother?

First, it makes the dog's gray matter work that much harder. That's to the good of all concerned. Second, it accents what "Fuss" actually means—that it refers to a specific location relative to you. Third, heightened canine focus: As the work is performed relative to you, the dog must concentrate on you. Last, it keeps your pet's attention on you after he arrives. He stays alert because you may next tell him to finish.[2]

Besides, the first time you show the exercise to your friends it'll knock their socks off. Look at your own reactions when you first saw it.

If you'd rather have your dog just come to you and go to heel in one motion, that's fine. It won't hurt a thing. But if you'd like to teach your pet the finish, let me show you how.

I borrow someone's dog and demonstrate how to teach the finish. I prefer the inside finish but occasionally I run into a dog who seems drawn toward the handler's right. From a canine perspective that can appear to be the heel side, even though the person is facing backward relative to the dog. With such an animal my approach is to accept success. I let him initiate to the side to which he seems more comfortable and teach the go-around finish. All we're after is the final result: the dog in the heel position. I tell the students this so that if an animal tends toward the go-around style the owner doesn't correct him.

Questions? Okay, get away from each other and try the finish a few times. Remember to praise "Good Fuss."

After allowing the students adequate time to work on the exercise, I call them together.

For now, don't tie the finish with the recall. That is, don't call your dog and—after he sits—tell him "Fuss." Keep the two exercises separate for a couple of weeks, or the animal may learn to return to heel without waiting for the command. He can see it as another automatic function, like auto-sit at heel and sitting front when coming to you.

Questions?

---

[2]As you probably know, the finish can also heighten bonding, but since the way the lesson does this is fairly abstract, I don't include it in the list.

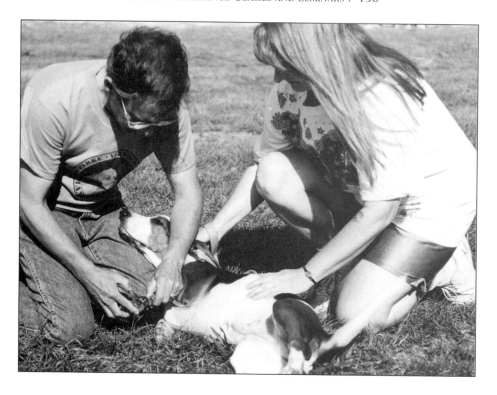

NAILS, EARS AND SUCH

Fearing they might cause bleeding, many owners are reluctant to trim nails. Also, students are often unaware of the need for periodic ear cleaning. During this class I demonstrate how to perform both tasks. Normally I use one of my own dogs for this "lesson," but if I'm unable to bring one of my pets I borrow a student's dog. I ask if the dog is a bleeder, but if I have any doubts as to the owner's knowledge I seek another dog.

After trimming and cleaning I demonstrate brushing. Then I discuss bathing, fleas, ticks, internal parasites and nutrition, and answer any questions that pertain.

Now, is all this "training"? Not really. So what's it doing in a basic Obedience class attended by people who, for the most part, aren't knowledgeable about canine grooming and upkeep? I see the question as being the answer.

After conducting this minisymposium on care and maintenance, I hand out the Week 4 sheets, thank everyone for coming and end the session.

REFLECTION

Animals are such agreeable friends—they ask no questions, they pass no criticisms.

—GEORGE ELIOT

Chapter 13

FIFTH WEEK

Okay, folks, form a circle, please. Any training problems or questions we need to hear about?

After dealing with whatever the students may have on their minds, we proceed with this graduation class.

Before showing you today's lessons, I want you guys to demonstrate what you and your dogs have learned. This is as close to a graduation ritual as I get. Each of you have obviously put a lot of time and effort into your project.

But I want to see how you're doing, so I'd like each of you to heel your dog through a weave.

"Say what?" typifies student reaction.

Well, we're in a large circle, yes? Four or five feet between each team. What you'll do—one at a time—is heel your dog throughout the group: In front of the first team you come to, behind the next one, in front of the one after that, and so on, until you return to your starting point.

I accompany the explanation by weaving throughout the group.

Now, when heeling your pet or while awaiting your turn, keep your leash slack but only to the extent that your dog has to work at staying with you. That is, don't let out more than a few inches of slack but do let out that much. When one dog approaches another, a tight leash can drive that dog toward the other. Let the control afforded by obedience hold the animal back but remember to keep your eyes on your dog. Your pet can look at another dog—that's normal behavior when one animal nears another—but don't allow pooch to take so much as one step toward another dog in the class.

Questions?

I field whatever is brought up and then continue.

After finishing the weave, heel your dog off to one side, leave him on a sit-stay, go to the end of your leash and call the animal. Then finish, and heel back to the group. Clear?

If there are no questions I outline another element.

We'll do stays in a group after everyone's done, but after each of you puts your pet through the heeling and recall/finish paces, then you'll have to endure—that is, you'll benefit from—a critique, not by me but by the toughest judges here: each other. As each team finishes up I want the rest of you to comment on what you saw, positive and negative. I'll throw my two cents in if needed but I'd rather you heard from each other.

Okay, who wants to volunteer to go first?

Someone may pipe up but if no one does I turn toward a person who I think has done well and "volunteer" that individual.

What's that? You say you can't wait to get started? Fine! I imagine everyone else will be bighearted and let you go first.

Of course, the person hadn't said a thing. This is just my way of using humor to break the ice, to at once get the proceedings off dead center while lessening student anxiety. Before this first individual starts, I speak to him or her.

When you're done and after the group has made its observations, you get to pick the next victim. Meantime, just forget the rest of us are here and go work your dog. It's just you and pooch. You'll do fine.

This routine is helpful in two respects. First, each student receives the benefit of observations other than mine. I don't claim to see all that happens, and this way each person gets the thinking of everyone present. Second, by "judging" others' performances, each student finds out what he or she has learned. It casts the observers into the role of teachers and as you may know, if you want to find out what you know about a subject, teach it. It can be a tremendous learning experience.

After the last performance we do a group sit-stay for a minute with the dogs scattered about the training area, and a group down-stay for several minutes.

A bugaboo that can occur pertains to the finish. The technical term is *anticipation*: in this case, someone's pet returning to heel before being commanded to do so.

Okay, the Golden finished on her own. She anticipated the command. Question: Should she be corrected?

Students often opine affirmatively.

I disagree. Look, we've taught these dogs to auto-sit at heel and to sit following a recall. Isn't it possible, even likely, that a bright dog might sense that the finish is another automatic function? I mean, study that Golden's expression. Do you see defiance? I don't.

"So what should a trainer do?"

Keep training. Step left and block the animal. Say "No" and pet the dog, to keep him or her in front of you. Break the pattern: Do two or three recalls without the finish. Correct for anticipation only when it's a defiant act.

Then I borrow someone's dog and move on to the first of today's lessons.

STAND-STAY

There's one form of stay that we've yet to teach these dogs. What is it?

Someone usually offers, "Standing?"

Right! And as we're using it here, the stand-stay is intended for grooming, not for use in a vet's office. I once watched a vet pulling porcupine quills from a dog's muzzle while the owner commanded the hapless animal, "Stay! Stay! Stay!" How to teach distrust in one easy lesson.

Anyway, let me borrow a dog and I'll show you how to teach the stand-stay.

After leading a dog a short distance from the group, I show him the lesson. Then I return dog to owner, ask the people what they saw, and cover any finer points that might have gone unnoticed.

Did anyone hear the command I used for the stand?

"I think you said 'Wait.'"

Right. You can use "Stand" if you'd rather but I use "Wait" because the "S" sound in "Stand" can cause a fast worker to ss-sit before you can stop him.

Two other points: First, don't heel your pet—that is, don't use "Fuss"—when moving him from place to place while teaching the stand. "Fuss" calls for an automatic sit when you stop and we're going for the stand right now, not the sit. Just tell pooch "C'mon" or the like.

Second, if your dog starts to sit, just move him a step or two and stand him again. Don't let him sit from the stand for now. These animals are very accustomed to sitting when they stop, so be patient. It might take a little time for them to get the idea of not sitting reflexively.

Questions?

If there are none I have the group work on "Wait" for a few minutes. Then I call everyone together.

HAND SIGNALS: HEELING, RECALL, FINISH

There are three hand signals I want to show you: Heeling, the recall and the finish. I've borrowed a dog here, and after moving him away from you guys I'll show him those signals. Now, watch what happens.

After working on the hand signals for as long as it takes to get the ideas into the dog's head, which is usually less than a couple of minutes, I return the animal to his owner and ask the students what they saw. Once it appears that the training techniques are clear to everyone I direct them to work on the signals for a few minutes. Then I call the group together for the final time.

People, before we leave I'd like to give you a few thoughts to take with you. The first has to do with stays. The question is, "How long is too long?" When I teach seminars, my dogs sometimes have to hold down-stays for over an hour while I'm working with students. No, the animals don't have to maintain an alert position; they can fall asleep if they wish. And I certainly wouldn't leave them in the sit or stand position for that long. That would be criminal. In everyday, around-the-house settings, if I need to leave my dog on a stay, I choose the one in which he'll be most comfortable. If I know that I'm going to be occupied for an extended period, I don't leave the dog on a stay at all. I cut him loose in the yard or put him in the house.

I pause for a moment for this to sink in. As I do, an often-asked question may be raised: "Do I keep working my dog even though these classes are over?"

You do, but you may no longer need to train every day. These dogs have learned a lot in five weeks but that doesn't mean they can't get better at what they already know. Besides, from what I've seen these past few sessions, they enjoy their training-time with you.

Someone usually confirms this: "When I get my dog's leash and collar out, he gets real excited. He's ready to go!"

Sure, and that's how it should be. His actions tell you that he likes working and, more important, he enjoys being with you.

Just as I always open beginner classes with, "Welcome to Dog Training 101," I have a way of ending a novice series.

There's one other area I want to get into before you leave. You've done well, not that you need me to tell you that. Your dogs' performances demonstrate what you've accomplished.

But there's a danger to training I want to caution you about: lost perspective. As you've seen, force is sometimes necessary in training. But it isn't an end in itself. I tell you this to warn you of an edge that I've known good people to topple over.

An inherent quality of training is control. It often sponsors the need. It also can be a trap, one that has throttled more than one relationship between dog and owner. You don't want to bury the dog's self or his identity in the name of training.

Don't start a session with an attitude of, "What will go wrong today?" Trainers should look for "What's right?" before "What's wrong?"

I tell you this only because the companionship of a good dog is without parallel. Sure, straight sits, fast recalls, tight heeling—all those things are important, but more so is the affection of your best friend.

Be careful. That's all I'm saying. Be careful.

I pause to let these thoughts percolate.

A continuation of this class is available. It has two basic goals: Distance control, such as being able to command the dog to "Platz" at increasing distances, and the beginnings of off-leash work, as in heeling and recalls. Like this class, the intermediate class runs for five weeks and the cost is the same. You can enroll today. There's not a dog here who isn't ready to continue.[1]

I go from student to student, giving each a Week 5 sheet, a diploma and a small paper sack containing a couple of dog biscuits, a rawhide strip or two and a few business cards.

Everybody, I want to thank you for taking my class. I'm flattered. I've made some friends here—two-legged and four-legged alike—and I've really enjoyed watching you and your pets learn. If I can be of any help to you in the future, please let me know.

Okay, that's it! Thanks again for coming! Good luck!

YOU MAY HAVE NOTICED . . .

I don't single out teams number one, two, three and so on. The practice tends to puff up a few folks while hurting everyone else's feelings. Each student signed up for different reasons and so long as they've met their goals, in my opinion no one should be told they didn't do as well as anyone else.

DIPLOMAS

Though diploma blanks can be had from various sources, I prefer the following sample which is of my own design. The symbols {FIELD}1~ through {FIELD}6~ are computer codes for WordPerfect's 5.1 program. This software allows me to insert a list, formatted as below, into the master document, which produces a diploma for each student.

{FIELD}1~   Dog's Name

{FIELD}2~   Breed of Dog

{FIELD}3~   Owner's Name

---

[1]That's not always true. In such cases the student seems to sense that he or she or pooch have gone as far as they can and simply don't enroll. Or, if the individual is unaware that more work is needed at the curent level, I have a private word with him or her, so as not to embarrass anyone.

{FIELD}4~   Day of Graduation

{FIELD}5~   Month of Graduation

{FIELD}6~   Year of Graduation

Joel M. McMains
Companion Obedience

**Certificate
of Completion**

𝕋his is to certify that

1~, a 2~

companion of

3~

has demonstrated the prescribed level of willingness, intelligence,

and understanding of the Dog Logic Companion Obedience Course,

and is therefore entitled to receive this

Diploma

Certified this 4~ day of 5~, 1997

Instructor

While *Teaching Obedience Classes and Seminars* is not about computer usage, I would be remiss were I not to mention that—through user-automated processes (known in computer terminology as *macros* or *batch files*)—only two keystrokes are needed to produce diplomas for an entire class, regardless of the number of students. Anyone familiar with word-processing software can devise any of several methods for creating such a system.

Diplomas for upper-level courses are identical to the foregoing, save for their titles of Intermediate, Advanced or Competition Preparation Obedience. For professional results, I use a laser printer and 24-pound, ivory-hued résumé paper to produce my diplomas. I sign each certificate above the word "Instructor."

REFLECTION

The dog is the god of frolic.

—HENRY WARD BEECHER

Part IV

CONTINUING
EDUCATION

Chapter 14

POST-NOVICE COURSES

This chapter covers my curricula beyond Companion Obedience. Each exercise is described but minute-by-minute narratives are not presented. That would be excessive, given the Companion-Obedience section's format. By now you should have a feel for my style of teaching.

I offer three levels of post-novice training: intermediate, advanced and competition preparation. Enrollment is restricted to graduates of the preceding course, except for approved handlers interested in my competition-preparation class.

Intermediate and advanced classes run for five weeks and tuition is the same as for my beginners course. Competition-preparation classes are billed quarterly at a lower cost per class. Competition-prep includes subclasses in retrieving, jumping and similar work pertaining to upper-level degrees.

ATTITUDE

Most successful first-time trainers who choose to further their learning make the transition smoothly, feeling their way along, deriving pleasure from new accomplishments and fresh insights, enjoying consequential heightened bonding. This is as it should be.

A minority, however, approach post-novice work from one of two equally hindering perspectives: "I can do it all!" or, "I can't do it at all." If you've been teaching classes for any length of time you've encountered both extremes. If you haven't, you will. In either case, instructors have an obligation toward both types of students and their dogs.

Overconfident students often develop tunnel vision. Having navigated the tides of novice obedience, they feel ready to train anything from movie dogs to police K-9s. As we know, those who believe that they've learned it all, whatever the field, may pay lip service to progress but actually make little sincere attempt to augment their knowledge. Thinking that there is nothing more to be mastered, they see only that which they feel they need to see.

These folks tune in on new lessons and applications, but references to "man's best friend" and the power of bonding seem to diminish in meaning for them. They correct for nit-picking faults and their praise loses spontaneity, becoming more mechanical than sincere. A gulf that had never existed between student and dog begins to widen.

Ironically, very often these trainers have made less headway than they believe. Armed with a pinch collar, a growing view toward pure control and a scant awareness of rapport's enhancing effects, they misread resignation and subjugation as indicative of thorough training.

Please, don't misunderstand: These are good people who have just become overzealous. Their perspective has become a tad skewed.

As an instructor, though you don't want anyone to lose his or her edge, you know excessive fervor can be dangerous, especially in terms of losing touch with one's pet. The novice who graduates too tightly wound may become fascinated with training's nuts and bolts to the exclusion of human-canine relationships, a misstep against which you must caution any student you feel needs it.

Now consider students at the attitudinal continuum's opposite end. They lack confidence, are hesitant and seem almost apologetic. "I've been able to teach pooch some on-leash stuff, but off-lead training is more than I can handle. Too much for my dog, too, I expect."

As mentioned in chapter 5, "Teaching Guidelines," "some folks need a little propping up from time to time." This is one such instance. While it may be alleged that we're flirting with some intimacy boundaries here, my thought is that sometimes a teacher should broach a topic not in the syllabus. Because the reality is that the student doesn't see that "I can't" concerns are dually flawed: They are both illogically founded and contrary to experience.

They are illogically founded because until a person has attempted beyond-the-basics training, he or she could have no notion of the difficulties (or lack thereof) entailed. They are contrary to experience because the overall message of having trained a dog through Companion Obedience is that both trainer and trainee have done well. Accomplishments in a previously foreign endeavor suggest that continued progress should ensue from graduate work. "Experience is the evidence."[1]

DRIVE TRAINING

As you will have gathered from the basic-obedience chapters, I root several early lessons in compulsion. This is because pet owners typically have neither time nor dedication for drive work. During upper-level classes, I show students how to use drive to enhance compulsion-based lessons. Further, I anchor much post-novice work in drive and reinforce it with compulsion as needed.

My goal is to help students produce reliable, happy workers. Thus, after first teaching each dog, "You must!" we teach him, "Now let me show you how much fun all this can be." Happy soon joins with reliable and the result is a self-perpetuating attitude whereby each mindset continually heightens the other.

Some students may tell you that their dogs have no interest in play objects and that drive training, therefore, has no function in their programs. Be sure the student knows what he or she is talking about. A friend once assured me that her Doberman had no interest in toys. I took the animal's leash, moved her away from the owner and tossed a tennis ball a few times. Sure enough, little more than a glance from the Doberman. So I flipped the pinch collar over, removing the pressure from pooch as the prongs were then pointing outward. I again enticed her with the ball and this time the animal exploded in happy pursuit.

While the methods you use for drive training are, of course, up to you, it is imperative they be included in continuing classes. To do otherwise is to neglect an essential facet of training. True, compulsion alone will produce basic obedience, and many pet owners aspire to no higher plateau than that; but linking compulsion and drive can produce awesome effects. Hence, drive work is crucial for students who wish to scale the heights of training and bonding. From the pen of Konrad Lorenz, "In every kind of training which demands active cooperation on the part of the dog, such as jumping, retrieving and other feats, we must

---

[1] *The Celestine Prophecy,* James Redfield (New York: Warner Books, Inc., 1993), 10.

not forget that even the best dog possesses no human sense of duty and, in sharp contrast to quite small children, will only collaborate as long as he is enjoying the work."[2]

INTERMEDIATE OBEDIENCE OUTLINE

EXERCISE	WEEK 1	WEEK 2	WEEK 3	WEEK 4	WEEK 5
Down at Distance	10 to 15 feet from sit	15 to 20 feet; add signal	20 to 30 feet from stand	30 to 40 feet	40 to 50 feet
Down from Motion	XXXX	Quick response	At fast walk	At quick jog	At full run
Recall Over High Jump	XXXX	XXXX	On-lead at 12 feet	Off-lead	Off-lead at 20 feet
Heel Off-Leash	XXXX	XXXX	XXXX	XXXX	Success for 15 feet
Recall Off-Leash	XXXX	XXXX	XXXX	From 10 feet	From 15 feet

ANALYSIS: INTERMEDIATE OBEDIENCE

Down at Distance refers to teaching pooch to hit the ground at ever-increasing distances from the handler, the idea being to extend control. The "Lie down" hand signal is added during the following session.

---

[2]Lorenz, Konrad, *Man Meets Dog* (New York: Kodanshin International, 1994).

Down from Motion is from the Schutzhund training regimen that teaches a dog to lie down during heeling; the handler does not break stride when commanding, "Platz." This is handier than the novice pattern of having to stop, then commanding the dog to "Down" and "Stay" before the owner can depart.

Recall Over High Jump is based in the novice recall and the over-jump-at-heel exercise. Useful for its own value, the lesson paves the way for off-leash work. It shows the dog to focus on taking the jump, not on whether he or she will come to the owner.

Heel Off-Leash and *Recall Off-Leash* are self-explanatory, both in purpose and usefulness.

ADVANCED OBEDIENCE OUTLINE

EXERCISE	WEEK 1	WEEK 2	WEEK 3	WEEK 4	WEEK 5
Sit from Down at Distance	At 10 feet; signal	At 20 feet	At 30 feet	At 35 feet	At 40 feet
Signals: Stand to Down to Sit to Recall	XXXX	At 10 feet	At 20 feet	At 25 feet	At 30 feet
Instant On	XXXX	XXXX	Quick response during play	Quick response during rest	Quick response around distractions
Guard Game	XXXX	XXXX	XXXX	Comprehension	Adapt to previous lessons
Tricks	XXXX	XXXX	XXXX	XXXX	Various

ANALYSIS: ADVANCED OBEDIENCE

The *Sit from Down at Distance* signal teaches a dog to sit from the down position at ever-increasing distances from the handler. Distance control and increased bonding are the motives for this and the following lesson.

Stand to Down to Sit to Recall via signals combines *Down at Distance* (from intermediate obedience) with the previous week's *Sit from Down at Distance,* and incorporates the signaled recall and finish from novice training's fifth week.

Instant On teaches pooch to respond to the sound of his name with flash attention on the trainer.

The *Guard Game* is a drive-based technique of my own creation that enhances working attitude while training a dog to focus concentration for prolonged periods, initially on a play object, ultimately on the trainer.

Training methods for the foregoing intermediate and advanced lessons appear in *Advanced Obedience—Easier Than You Think.*

Tricks is self explanatory. This session is a series favorite for students and instructors alike. Training techniques appear in *Dog Logic—Companion Obedience.*

DISTRACTIONS

You'll recall from novice chapters such proofing techniques as heeling dogs past one another, and students requiring their pets to remain sitting at heel during simulated meetings of friends. As part of intermediate and advanced instruction I offer at least one new distraction-conditioning method or conceptual enhancement weekly. Any of the following can be conducted on- or off-leash, depending on the handler's awareness and the dog's reliability, though a collar tab should be attached for safety.

Corridor heeling/recalls entail performing both exercises between two facing lines of students whose dogs should remain sitting at heel. The corridor's width should be at least eight feet and the distance between student-dog teams should never be so slight as to risk a dogfight. Though students forming the corridor should initially ignore the animal being worked, this proofing technique can be heightened in many ways, such as having facing students roll or toss a ball back and forth as the dog nears, or even beckoning to the animal by name.[3]

---

[3]Family members should not call to the dog, of course, nor should any person who is well known to the animal.

"Pressure-cooker" heeling.

A similar setup is *crowd heeling*, which is heeling a dog through a moving crowd of people, in this case students. Unlike the Schutzhund exercise on which this conditioning is based, the people forming the crowd may have their dogs with them, or the animals can be holding stays a short distance away.

Other heeling-recall variations include practice on stairways, through doorways and gates, and among parked cars. This conditioning should take place at the class site, not at shopping centers or other unsafe locations.

Another effective conditioner goes like this. Toward the end of the allotted class time, tell the students they are about to get a shot at acting. Have everyone take their pets to the parking area (or at least away from the building, if you're teaching indoors), put each animal in its owner's car, as though it's time to go home, wait a few seconds, then heel back to the training site for a few more minutes of practice. The illusion the students create is that class is over. The reality is that the dog's obedience is never suspended; it is always available.

My favorite conditioning tactic is having one dog at play, such as chasing a tennis ball or Frisbee, while the rest of the class works. Every few minutes the dog being allowed to play rejoins the working animals and one of the latter takes the place of the former.

Of course, the question arising from the foregoing is, Which distractions should be used during which sessions? And I can't define that because, as suggested earlier, each class—like each student—is different in terms of how much it can handle. For some advanced groups, having one dog at play while the others work is too much, while some intermediate classes can deal with it effortlessly.

If recall enthusiasm could be put on a scale, this little dog's fire would be found to outweigh his light-line.

COMPETITION PREPARATION COURSE

As mentioned earlier, few students who take a "basic" class do so motivated by a desire to participate in competition. This bent continues to be seen during initial post-novice courses. Many students want only to continue their pets' training and their personal educations. During intermediate and advanced series, however, I sporadically allude to this or that aspect of competition, principally AKC or Schutzhund Obedience.

As you might suspect, via my interjections I'm trolling for potential competitors, whetting the appetites of those for whom Obedience competition has intrinsic appeal. These folks are seeking something beyond practical applications of their dogs' training. It is to them that I offer competition-preparation classes.

My competition-prep instructional approach differs from conventional teaching practice in two major respects. First, though I initially point competition students toward the CD, that does not remain their sole focal point. We also work on elements appertaining to CDX and UD titles and to Schutzhund Obedience.

My reasoning for this teaching strategy is, first, when all is said and done, the CD routine is neither complex nor arduous. By taking Companion Dog contenders past the degree's requirements before they ever set foot in a Novice ring, attaining the title becomes much easier. Second—and this is closely related to the foregoing—given the relative ease of completing a CD title, the routine can become more than a trifle colorless for handlers and dogs alike. By interpolating other lessons into what is ostensibly a CD prep class, interest is kept at a higher level.

Exceptions to this guideline relate to the Open drop on recall and Utility recall to heel: The drop should not be shown to a Companion Dog candidate until the title has been secured. Likewise, the UD exercise should not be taught to a pre-CDX animal. Stress can affect performance, and a dog who has been prematurely taught the drop or the recall to heel might do so out of confusion or nervousness when working in the semistressful environment of a dog show.

Otherwise, so long as a lesson has no potential for conflict or confusion with requirements of uncompleted titles, there is no harm but there are many benefits in teaching CDX, UD and Schutzhund Obedience to a pre-Novice dog. By basing instruction on what each dog and trainer can handle, irrespective of the titles currently pursued, exhibitors have a better shot at success.

A month or so before shows students have entered, I suspend introduction of new lessons for those people and their dogs. I don't start focusing exclusively on routines pertaining to the titles sought, but I do call a temporary halt to commencing new work. This is to settle and order the handlers' and dogs' minds, which new lessons can disrupt.

COMPETITION PREPARATION OUTLINE

I don't have one. A competition-prep outline, I mean. Because every group's state of readiness is different, I teach to the level of each class, approaching each series from a slightly different angle. As the dogs have the training and the handlers start with at least a notion of CD requirements, having heard my earlier-mentioned comments about competition, my purpose is to fill in the blanks. To follow a schematic calling for practicing this or that aspect during this or that week would be to ignore the human and canine factors as they pertain to learning potential.

The key here is personalized instruction. At competition level, not only do most students seem more comfortable with this kind of teaching technique, it achieves better results than do blueprinted courses. I've seen attempts at reducing competition training to a fold-tab-A-into-slot-B process; while I've never been fond of the method, I have been bored stiff by it.

COMPETITION PREPARATION INSTRUCTION

My foundation classes—basic, intermediate and advanced—cover the same material in every series. Each course has clear lines of beginning and ending. My competition-prep classes are based on students' stated interests and my reading of their dogs' reliability. Also, as these classes are ongoing, they can be entered at any time by graduates of my foundation classes, or by experienced handlers.

I furnish each student with the judge's sheet relevant to the title sought. Together we analyze these forms' content in depth until the students are fully conversant with the interpretation of each component. I also provide the addresses where students can write for AKC Obedience Trial regulations and for Schutzhund regulations, for those who are interested. I require that each student send for the material on his or her own and become familiar with it. I could easily furnish these booklets myself but I want the students to take the initiative for this part of their instruction as preparation for their taking the initiative in later stages of the training they and their dogs will undergo.

Along with shoring up any weak areas of training, usually byproducts of canine immaturity, my competition-preparation classes accent four themes: new material, polishing, conditioning and ring and trial-field handling.

NEW MATERIAL

This relates to exercises new to handlers and dogs. The figure eight is one example, the stand for examination another. I base lesson selection and sequencing on class composition. As mentioned earlier, an underlying design of competition training is to keep student and canine interest high.

POLISHING

Polishing is one-third of my training method: Teach approximates, then polish, then condition. When teaching a dog new work, I show her what she needs to know to respond as best as she's able to the ideal I have in mind. How close each dog initially comes to the bull's-eye is a function of the individual dog's talent and temperament and my training prowess.

Especially with early lessons, canine responses are often less than flawless; but to criticize when an animal is giving her best would be to risk knocking down attitude and morale. Thus, my philosophy is to accept the animal's best for what it is, her current best, and then to polish her responses until they parallel my standards.

Now, reread the preceding two paragraphs and substitute *student* for each reference to man's best friend, and you'll see how I approach the job of helping trainers to bring their pets to their individual levels of performance excellence. Like dogs, people can improve only so much at one time. I never hold a student back or accept mediocre efforts gladly, but I also know that people (and dogs) learn better over time than from crash courses.

On the subject of polishing: I don't hold that automatic sits, for example, have to be accurate to within a tiny fraction of an inch. I take such precision when it comes my way but I don't expect it of each and every dog. Some breeds, and some animals within breeds, perform with exactitude more naturally than do some others. It's not my role to fiddle with or judge creation but to work with what's at the other end of the leash.

In sum, I guide each team toward what I perceive as its particular zenith, ever mindful that creating a dispirited, furry robot is never an option. More than anything I want to see dog and handler in tune, each giving his or her best, canine reliability being a given. Second-best performances by owner or ownee are never condoned but neither are they condemned. They are simply the best the handler or the dog could do at the time.

CONDITIONING

Each competition-prep meeting is something of a mini dog show. If a lower-level class precedes the competition session, I invite the students to stick around for as much of the competition meeting as they can. Precompetition folks working their pets near the ring area, loudly visiting with each other, dropping metal folding chairs nearby and shouting to their friends—generally being distractive—can provide realistic ring conditioning.

When students bring children to class I enlist their efforts too (but only with their parents' permission, of course). "Kids, this is a tennis ball. That is a training ring." Pretty soon the youngsters are playing catch near the ring, yelling to one another, running about the ring's perimeter and so on.[4]

Radios blaring, an occasional small firecracker set off a good distance from the dogs, one dog being recalled along a line between handlers and dogs during stays (to simulate an animal running loose in a ring) and similar distractions are periodic parts of the scene. To list all conceivable distractive influences would be an Herculean task and besides, I imagine you have many of your own personal favorite distraction techniques.

My criteria for effective ring conditioning is threefold: fair, nonharmful and real-world. Fair in the sense that no distraction should appear threatening to a dog. That no distraction should be potentially harmful is self-evident. "Real-world" excludes such absurdities as having a family member call to a dog while the animal is being worked. I've seen classes wherein heavy-duty firecrackers were ignited within a few feet of animals who were taken to task if they broke their obedience in response. That violates all three rules and teaches associated environmental (ring) anxiety.

HANDLING

Regardless of a dog's depth of training, successful outings seldom occur when linked to submarginal handling. I carry indelible memories—one of a competitor in the Novice class asking a judge, "You mean we have to heel off-leash, too?" another asking, "What do you mean by *finish?*", a third who was so nervous she didn't notice until she'd "heeled" several feet that her dog had left the ring and she was performing solo, people who give multiple commands as a matter of course and others who show up in a drug-induced haze—all are examples of destructive handling, to say the least (and, in many cases, certain to be blamed on the dog after the fact). True, the foregoing presents varying extremes of ineptitude, but we've all seen (and perhaps experienced) points lost and qualifying scores slipped away, the result of handler errors. While blunders can result from

---

[4]Of course, never allow children to be put in harm's way, such as by running back and forth near dogs on stays.

simple nervousness, the origins of such can more often be traced to careless practice. Examples:

- students chatting with one another
- students changing their own body positions during stays
- handlers muttering to themselves or to the person playing the judge during heeling.
- Students allowing (or even encouraging) their pets to jump on them between exercises.

I imagine you get the idea and could add to this list. The point is that people do what they're accustomed to doing in a specific situation. This is especially true when students are under stress. That's when folks subconsciously fall back on comfortable habits to seek security from the strain. A person who has practiced responding (or not responding) in a certain way is likely to respond similarly when the heat's on. Hence:

People, practice it the way you're going to do it, until your responses become reflexive. That way, when in the ring, you won't have to think about how to respond. The good habits you're building will take over and see you through.

CONTRACT

My competition students and I honor a four-part pact. One and two, I will teach them everything I know about their area of interest, and will do all I can to help them reach their goals. Three, they don't participate in fun matches wherein pinch collars, corrections and praise during exercises are not allowed. The purpose of entering a match is not to win the event or even to place—that's just gravy—the idea is to ring-condition the dog and the handler. Fourth, no student enters a real show until we both agree that owner and dog are ready. Until both members of a team are prepared they have no business in actual competition. All that does is waste entry fees and judges' time.

THE TOUGHEST JUDGES

Students can give each other valuable insights. Because they've yet to enter a competition ring, or have done so probably with far less frequency than you have, they may sense problem areas that you yourself once experienced but have forgotten. Ergo, once a class achieves a state wherein an adequate number of students and their dogs are becoming proficient at a given competition level, ask one or more different students every week to play the role of judge and ask all students for observations.

MISDIRECTED FOCUS

The following is intended mainly for Novice "A" competitors.

Old-fashioned merry-go-rounds offered riders a chance to grab a brass ring from a mechanical holder mounted along the circumference. Winners earned a free ride and, of course, a shot at another brass ring.

Occasionally a rider, in reaching for the ring, would lose his or her balance and fall from the horse. Injuries sometimes resulted, ambulance-chasing lawyers converged like vultures and soon the "brass ring" come-on bit the dust.

A second problem derived from the fact that no one can be in two places at once, physically or psychologically. Some folks, when leaving the merry-go-round, felt neither exhilarated nor elated but let down. Preoccupied in their brass-ring quest, which was often unsuccessful (as the gimmick's designers intended), they missed the fun of the ride.

Now, apply that bit of arcade arcana to concepts like "First Place" and "High in Trial" and you'll understand the title of the subhead for this section. A success ratio exceeding 95 percent at any task is pretty darn good, yet I've heard competitors who scored in the mid-190s pronounce their day a shambles because they didn't finish atop the heap (or, just as often, because someone else did). Sure, such laments—"We only scored 196!"—are sometimes a back-door way of strutting, but when folks make such statements in earnest, they belittle not just their own achievements (and that of their dogs), they miss the ride.

Granted, my brass-ring analogy is somewhat flawed: High in Trial, First Place, a 200 score—those are hardly synonymous with brass rings. Any or all are magnificent accomplishments of which any competitor should be proud. In terms of earning a title, however, remember that "qualifying score" is the magic phrase. Many people never get that far. Besides, if one person earns a title with scores of 190-something and a second individual averages 171, they both win the same degree.

"Agreed. But didn't the 190-plus exhibitor do better than someone who barely squeaked through?"

Maybe. Some breeds carry a multipoint handicap every time they enter a ring. That is, if I train and show a Sheltie, I expect to qualify in three straight shows with scores well above 190. With certain other breeds, three scores above 170 during the dog's lifetime will be fine.

MISCONCEPTION

You may have the impression that my competition-prep classes are less formally structured than those covering foundational obedience. That's an illusion, one I purposefully create. I know exactly where everyone's education is going, and am continually several lesson-stages ahead of each team.

My classes aren't hard-driving or intense. Though I recognize that some people are uncomfortable when operating at less than warp speed, I don't push a go-go attitude onto students. Other than the obvious goal of ring-refining handlers, dogs and obedience generally, my aims are to help folks maintain perspective and cope with anxiety. First, perspective:

There's something I tell my 4-H students: Anyone who puts sincere effort into training and showing shouldn't assume blame if things don't go well. Best is best, and it's difficult to rehearse for all that can happen at a dog show. A nonqualifying score or last-place finish doesn't imply that handler or dog is a loser; they are just more experienced.

By the same sign, a professional exits the ring without sharing disappointments with his canine teammate. Dogs aren't constituted to handle human emotional loads. Negative vibes teach only nervousness. When I overhear, "My dog let me down," I feel sorry for the animal. I'm not suggesting he comprehends the words but surely he understands the tone. (It's also tempting to remind the speaker that it was he or she who trained the dog, obviously not too well.) Win, lose or draw, make sure your pooch knows he's always your companion, that he's ever your number one.

Regarding anxiety: Look, AKC requirements are rigid but they're manageable. Sure, incomplete training or inappropriate conditioning will generally have the predictable effect of scores below 170, as will competing a dog ill-suited to the work at hand. But what sinks many exhibitors is tension born of fear, the catchphrase for which is *ring nerves*. That's why much of what I try to teach competition students is how to relax, how to control the effects of stress.

People, I don't know that I've ever met a judge who I thought was officiating hoping to flunk anyone. They've all had to compete successfully and build qualifications to become Obedience judges and they know that you may be nervous.

The reality is that a certain degree of anxiety is normal. If you weren't somewhat atwitter I'd be worried about you.

What you need to see is how to make tension work for instead of against you. It's your nervousness, so learn to control it rather than allowing it to control you.

- *Forget the other rings. Concentrate only on the one you're in.*

- *Use your mind to tune out the crowd. Learn to ignore the audience to the extent that, in effect, it's not there.*

- *Shut out the noises. Don't hear them. Distraction-proof yourself as thoroughly as you do your dog.*

- *Operate only in the now. Forget about yesterday and tomorrow. One's as gone as anything can be; the other will get here soon enough. Thoughts about either can only distract you from what you're doing.*

- *And make that "operate only in the right now." Don't think even about the next exercise. Concentrate just on what you're doing at the moment.*

- *Focus solely on your dog and the judge's instructions. Nothing else matters. Nothing else exists.*

- *Don't analyze what's happening. Just perform.*

And enjoy. Above all, enjoy.

REFLECTION

Fear is the main source of superstition and one of the main sources of cruelty. To conquer fear is the beginning of wisdom.

—BERTRAND RUSSELL

Chapter 15

SEMINARS

I've never presented two identical seminars. Perhaps neither will you. Variables inherent to workshops should preclude carbon-copy presentations. Just as the cities you visit are similar yet different, the situations and training needs you'll face will be alike yet distinct. The students' knowledge, their experiences with other trainers, their training and teaching problems—all combine to create a new/old mosaic of each stop along the way.

From page one of *Dog Logic—Companion Obedience:* "I don't teach from a script." Though my reference was local classes, I approach seminars similarly. The key to presenting an effective, useful clinic is in juxtaposing students' accomplishments against their training objectives, and in helping them see how to attain their goals.

I've attended workshops where students' concerns were peripheral. A show was put on, and while some of the material may have been useful, hours were squandered. Either the students and their dogs were at a training level beyond the lessons given, or vice-versa, and/or their problems were not addressed. Hence, my disdain for choreographed clinics.

Therefore, while this chapter does not specify how to conduct a seminar minute-to-minute, it offers guidelines for putting on a successful clinic. How I commence the proceedings is covered—I have a definite way of getting things rolling—but from that point I respond to students' training needs. The seminar is theirs, not mine. It is to serve them, not me.

Though similar to running Obedience classes, seminar work is markedly different. Understanding and appreciation of those differences, and—more to the point—how to manage them, plus certain dos, don'ts and think-about-its, comprise much of this section's focus.

IS IT FOR YOU?

That's the first consideration. Are you comfortable working in unfamiliar settings with people and dogs new to your acquaintance? Is travel a problem for you? Can you accept skepticism, and minds that sometimes read *closed?*

Consider, too, you may encounter trainers whose knowledge is on a par with your own and may even surpass it. Can you handle that? I've seen instructors who were discomfited in such circumstances. They seemed to feel threatened and became defensive, losing sight of the fact that there is always someone who knows more, and this in no way diminishes their personal accomplishments, worth or right to be there. Their anxiety led to closing off, to forgetting that a steady response would have been to listen up and learn.

Another thought concerns the reality that, just as sometimes there seems to be an inexorable progression from trainer to teacher, some Obedience-class instructors buy into the notion that seminar work must follow. Many learn they not only aren't cut out for the job, they discovered it the hard way.

They have the knowledge, and they're good teachers, but being away from their home turf makes them feel too ill-at-ease to conduct an effective workshop. Does this make them lesser-thans? Of course not. Non sequitur time. It just means that seminar work isn't right for them at their present level of development.

Listen, if you've never had the experience, it can be quite a feeling to be introduced as an expert to a roomful of strangers, and presented with a problem foreign to your ken. Thoughts like, "Well, er, ah, I, that is, you see, I, uh," can arise.

Still, outlook is the key. I've yet to meet a seminar instructor who hasn't experienced a "Hhhmmmm!" episode of problem solving, and most of us took the challenge for what it was. We realized that the answer was there—that we just hadn't seen that particular puzzle before—and that if we'd listen to the dog he'd supply the answer. We worked through the situation to the satisfaction of all concerned and we learned along with our audience.

In overall terms, I've found that if teaching classes is fun, teaching clinics is a gas! For me, *challenging* and *rewarding* describe seminar work. Challenging, as I may run into problems new to my experience, allowing me to probe my "think-dog" capabilities. Challenging in that, while I have weeks to figure out a local Obedience-class dog, during a clinic I may have but minutes. Rewarding because I'm able to meet many good people and dogs and to expand my knowledge. Rewarding also in that I have opportunities to work with very skillful trainers while visiting places I might not see otherwise.

Of greatest personal importance, I'm able to refute some of the more heavy-handed training systems, to offer my more down-to-earth approach, to demonstrate there are better ways.

And the icing on the cake is that people are willing to pay me to do all this!

Negatives? Sure, there are a few. Travel can be a pain. And oxymorons like *restaurant food* and *hotel living* can quickly get old. But then, if you live in a snow-belt, there are worse fates than Dixie seminars in January.

POLICIES AND PRACTICES

Your phone rings. The caller represents a group interested in sponsoring a seminar. Long before this happy moment occurs, resolve several pertinent issues, not the least of which is the basis for and amount of your fee. Now, just as it's your place to set your own charges, you must also determine your terms and conditions. The best I can offer is to spell out my requirements so you can be sure to address the same issues in the way that works best for you.

As my clinics are usually two-day events, I try to confine them to weekends, from 9 A.M. to 6 P.M. on both days with an hour for lunch. Saturday evenings often find me spending time with students, talking dogs if not actually training.

My fee is based on the number of students. If the sponsors wish to charge more to try for a profit, that's up to them.

An alternative plan is to charge a set amount, irrespective of how many folks attend. I base my fee on the number enrolled simply because I seem to get more business by telling organizers that my charge is per student versus per seminar.

My clinics are limited to thirty-five people with dogs. I wouldn't insist a thirty-sixth team be turned away, but I want to have sufficient time for hands-on with each animal and work meaningfully with each owner.

My minimum number of students is twenty. That's not to say I won't teach a seminar of nineteen, but I've found that a significantly lesser number doesn't afford adequate compensation.

I have no limit for the number attending without dogs but my charge is the same as for those with dogs. I'm selling knowledge, and regardless of whether a student brings a dog, he or she has access to the same information as any other attendee.

Fees must be received by me at least three weeks before the clinic and are nonrefundable. Some organizations send me each student's personal check (rather than depositing the checks and sending me one drawn on the club's account), and three weeks may be needed for checks to clear.

I cover my own expenses, such as travel, lodging, meals and so forth. Sponsors are responsible for advertising and for providing a meeting place and equipment such as jumps and floor mats. Audio and video taping of my seminars is permitted but distributing copies of those materials is not.

Each person must complete my standard Enrollment form and sign my Agreement. (Sample forms appear in chapter 2, "Simplicity.")

I reserve the right to decline to work any dog present. This proviso is for extreme cases wherein an animal has bitten everyone in the family twice and half the neighborhood at least once. I'm not in this business to risk being ripped up by overly aggressive lost causes.

FLYERS

Have a supply of fully-informative flyers printed. Not only are they useful in outright solicitation, it's just good business to follow up inquiries by sending written material. Sure, you'll discuss essentials over the phone, but help yourself by mailing each caller something he or she can read and circulate among others in their respective clubs. This puts material with your name on it in the caller's hands and reinforces the fact that you welcome the group's business.

PLAN AHEAD

You've made commitments and received payments for a seminar. What to do next? Make your travel plans. Whether you intend to drive, fly or go by bus, train or pogo stick, and whether you're going to stay in a hotel or with friends, make all necessary reservations well in advance. Also, secure written confirmations for all reservations, and note the names of the people with whom you make those arrangements.

The need for travel and hotel reservations is obvious, but what can be overlooked is that if you plan to drive, make sure your vehicle is in sound mechanical condition. No one ever needs a breakdown; you sure don't need one when you're en route to honor a commitment. Also, plan your route and allow extra time for road construction and any other unforeseeable obstacles.

Make a checklist of training equipment, supplies and personal items you'll need. It does your aura of authority no good to be before a group and find you forgot to pack an essential piece of equipment. Sure, mistakes happen and people are generally understanding, but the effect can still dampen your presentation.

Schedule travel-recovery time. Jet lag or a long day behind the wheel can take the oomph out of anyone, and a tired instructor does not for an effective seminar make.

A seemingly minor specific is this: Pack an alarm clock. Motels usually remember requested wake-up calls; but time-zone changes can disrupt your internal clock and should someone forget to call you and you oversleep . . . well, you get the idea.

Record pertinent expenses and obtain receipts. If you drive, note your mileage and keep track of seminar-related automotive costs.

If you travel to greatly different climates, bring proper attire. I know an Arizona gent who did a May seminar in the northern Rocky Mountain region. My friend overlooked that springtime in the Rockies can differ vastly from the same season in Phoenix. The upshot was that he found himself driving in a nasty snowstorm and frigid temperatures, but had packed only lightweight clothing.

TO BRING OR NOT TO BRING?

Do you intend to take one or more of your dogs? If so, and if you're flying, are you aware of "minimum weather conditions" regulations? If temperatures at the departing or arriving airports are above or below certain levels at flight time, your animals may not be allowed to board. That can result in an official saying moments before departure time that your pets cannot be boarded, and you with no way of getting them home before the plane leaves.

I don't airship my dogs—not just to seminars, for any reason. That's partly due to the "minimum weather conditions" rule. It's also because I've heard too many horror stories about things going wrong vis-à-vis pets shipped by air. Such tales approximate, "That critter just hasn't been right since I flew him." That is, no one knows what went wrong, just that something did—big time. When I contract for a faraway seminar, I either drive or leave my dogs at home, usually the former.

Along with making sure your pet is currently vaccinated, know that bringing a dog may necessitate obtaining a veterinarian's health certificate, including proof of rabies vaccination, for interstate travel. Determine well ahead of time the applicable regulations for the areas you'll be traveling through and to. If in doubt, secure a health certificate.

A related consideration concerns where you plan to stay. If you are moteling it, ascertain when making your reservation that the inn will accept your dog(s). The time to discover a *No Pets!* rule is not when you're checking in. Moreover, get it in writing. Insist a note appear on your reservation confirmation that your animals may stay *in your room,* not in your car or in an area boarding kennel.

Bring a first-aid kit, dog food and a supply of drinking water. The water may be from your own tap at home or bottled spring water and is for your dog, not you. Changing water from locale to locale can produce a remarkable case of the "trots." Adding a dash of ReaLemon to pooch's drinking supply can be a preventative, but bringing water from home is safer yet.

Are you traveling with a protection animal? If so, advise the housekeeping department that staff members should not enter your room unless you and your dog are elsewhere.

Another worthwhile caution is securing the name and telephone number of a nearby veterinarian. You may not need a vet's services but such preparation comes under the heading "An ounce of prevention . . . ," and can save precious time in an emergency.

All that said, the main issue is still whether to bring one or more of your dogs. The question to ask yourself is: Will my dog's presence benefit the people attending my seminar? In most instances the answer will be yes.

Your dogs' performances validate that your training is productive, that it works. Further, while you should be able to clear up students' problems pertaining to the basics quickly, you may not be able to take someone's dog from CD to CDX level in a day or two. Having your dog with you facilitates demonstration of finer points that a student's pet may not be ready to internalize swiftly.

Downside: Much of the experience may be a study in boredom for your dog. Mine often "hold" two-hour down-stays (during which they sleep, which is fine) while I teach. Periodically I tell the group, "We've been going at it for well over an hour now and if you'll excuse me for a couple of minutes, I'd like to let my dog know I haven't forgotten him." I then spend a few moments with the animal, petting and telling him how good he's doing, apologizing for the monotony and perhaps taking him for a brief walk.

When I bring one of my dogs I try to arrange to have a friend travel with me (covering the individual's expenses, of course). This provides my pet with the company of someone he knows during the long hours when I need him nearby for impromptu demonstrations, but not right next to me.

As the person accompanying is usually a trainer familiar with my methods, I have a sounding board for feedback during breaks about points I might have overlooked or not spent enough time on. To teach a seminar is to work under time constraints, and it's not difficult to omit an element you know so well that you've forgotten you know it. That can lead to presuming your audience knows and understands a given concept when in truth the people have never heard of it. The result, of course, would be faulty communication and short-changed students.

SOMETHING ELSE TO PACK

Your sense of humor. No, I don't imply you should have a routine of ribald humor and political jokes. You're there to teach and train, but—though it may come as a shock to some—you're also there to entertain. People want to have fun during a clinic. They want to learn but they also want to kick back and have a good time.

The eminent trainer/author Carol Lea Benjamin once told me, "Once I hear that first laugh, I know it's going to be okay." I imagine you know what she meant. Regardless of how comfortable you are in your knowledge and motivation, slight nervousness when first addressing a new group is only human. But once you hear the common connection of humorous laughter over something you've said or done, you relax and so do the students. They may be anxious, too. Many may be concerned their dogs are going to "do something" in the presence of an expert. Laughter informs both sides that contact has occurred, communication has begun. This lightens the load for everyone.

TAKE FIVE . . .

. . . or ten. That is, at least every couple of hours, take a break. You'll not only need one, your students will. As teaching tires an instructor, learning wears on students. People can take in only so much at a time without becoming mentally fatigued. Just as it's helpful to pause for a few seconds after making a major point, to give it time to sink in, it's useful to stop for several minutes during a series of major presentations for the same reason.

A SELDOM-MENTIONED POINT

Are you a smoker? If so, it's not my place to dissuade you but I suggest you refrain while teaching. Not only do many folks object to secondhand fumes, tobacco smoke can be distractive to people and dogs alike. I once watched a gifted, knowledgeable trainer lose points hourly during a seminar as he perpetually had a cigarette in hand or sticking out of his mouth, usually the latter, even when working dogs. More than once during breaks, student discussions centered not on the individual's brilliant training acumen and dynamic techniques, but, "I wish he'd get rid of that filthy cigarette!"

BEFORE CLOSING

It's simple courtesy to acknowledge the many people who have expended much time and effort to plan, arrange, promote and assist during the clinic. Before closing the workshop, single out those who were instrumental and direct the well-deserved applause their way. Then thank all who attended. Without them, you wouldn't have been asked there to begin with.

I've yet to teach a workshop whose sponsors didn't ask me back. My practice of thanking all concerned, and pointing out to the group that during the clinic I've experienced some learning myself, which is always the case, may be two reasons why.

COMPONENTS

My seminars are composed of eight parts: (1) survey of students and dogs, (2) basic training, (3) training philosophy, (4) compulsion and drive, (5) distraction conditioning, (6) advanced training, (7) competition and (8) problem solving. As you'd expect of any integrated program, each element relates to others in varying degrees. As I finish one component I don't chop it off, never to refer to it again. Were that the case my presentations would be disjointed rather than coherent.

SURVEY

To give fair value you must first assess students' progress, determining points from which to proceed with each person. Just as practicing stays with dogs who are rock solid is pointless, there's little merit in trying to teach directed jumping to animals who have never seen a high jump.

I use three forms of screening. First:

People, I need to see where you and your dogs are in your training. So before we get underway would you heel your pets around the area for a few minutes? I won't run you through a pattern of "Forward, Right Turn, Halt," and so forth. Just heel your dogs on your own, on-leash or off, whichever you feel good about, and let's see what we've got here.

Of course, by virtue of student participation we indeed "get underway." The seminar is now cooking, everyone has eased into the water, and the focus is where it belongs: on the students and their dogs.

I've long felt that heeling—precision heeling, now not just ring-acceptable—is the most difficult basic to refine. The dog who heels well is usually not just past contention but is reliable at other fundamentals.

Heeling—excellent, woeful or somewhere in between—also can indicate the communication level a handler has achieved with his or her pet. I've yet to see top-notch heeling in the absence of sound rapport. Mechanical, stay-at-the-owner's-side heeling, yes, often complimented by ears laid back, plastered tail and intense, nervous concentration. But relaxed, in-tune heeling—that takes bonding.

So in this first evaluative step I'm looking for two things: Which dogs are how adept at heeling? And, at what level is the human-canine relationship between each trainer and dog? After watching enough heeling to allow me to form sufficiently valid opinions, I ask students to recall their pets over a standard high jump and then do a finish (or, with those dogs unschooled in jumping, do a normal recall and finish).

My third tactic is to move through the group, saying "Hi" to each owner and petting every dog. As you doubtless know, you can tell much about a dog by watching him perform basic Obedience; but you can tell more, especially about temperament and attitude, by briefly visiting with the animal.

BASIC TRAINING

I've yet to teach a seminar that didn't have at least one very green dog present. Usually, in fact, there are several. These dogs strain against leashes during heeling, have only the vaguest notion about "Sit" (let alone automatic-sit at heel), and "Stay" has little meaning for them. I seek out such a critter, ask to borrow him briefly, walk the animal to a location where all can see and commence as follows.

We need to start at square one so I can show you my approach to basic training. Otherwise, were I to begin with a more experienced dog, you'd miss out on how I establish foundational lessons. Later, when covering an advanced point that derives from one of those lessons, it might not be clear what I'm getting at. This dog's training hasn't been as extensive as that of some others here. I'm going to work with him for a few minutes—I won't be talking to you while I do that; my focus will be on the dog—then I want you to tell me what you saw.

Within minutes the dog is heeling, auto-sitting at heel, and able to hold a strong enough sit-stay that he'll resist very slight leash pressure to move from position. With the animal's tail at full wag, I return to the group and ask, "What did you see?"

Often I'm greeted with some chins on the floor, many smiles, savvy old-timers (which doesn't necessarily translate into *old folks*) grinning and nodding sagely, and an amazed owner. "You've gotten more out of my dog in a few minutes than I've been able to in a month."[1]

That's kind of you to say—I appreciate it—but it isn't the point. Virtually anyone can learn how to do this. I wasn't born with the knowledge. I've learned it, just as you can, and will.

The typical dog doesn't need to be shown a given thing several hundred times for it to sink in. One to four times is more like it. You have to remember that in the wild, the dog's natural setting, he might have but a single learning opportunity to avoid winding up in another animal's stew pot. Thus, nature has programmed him to learn quickly and thoroughly.

When I see a trainer showing a dog something over and over and over, often I see a burned-out dog. And the real trouble is repetition commonly sends the wrong message: that the trainer will always do the work for the dog, by placing him in position or making him heel or whatever. The animal is never told, "You must do this," which is much of what training is: showing the dog that he has to do what he's been taught.

I told this dog "Sit" and simultaneously showed him, "You have to do it." I told him to heel while sending the same "You must!" message. I handled "Stay" similarly.

Now, did I lose attitude in the process? Did all this knock pooch down? I think not. Look at that tail action, and how he's looking up at me. I see a happy dog. Already we're buddies. I'm taking his nervous, undirected energy and channeling it toward what we want: obedience. We're giving this pack animal a pack leader. That's something he not only understands but craves.

All you have to know are a few basic mechanics and concepts to get quick, long-lasting results. Let me return this fine dog to his owner and then let's talk about pinch collars.

---

[1] Has this start-up demonstration ever backfired, leaving me with an unwilling dog who wouldn't do anything I tried to show him? No. I can read *Canis familiaris,* and I presume you've developed the same skill else you'd not be teaching seminars.

I had slipped a pincher on the dog after moving him away from his owner. Now, after outlining why I prefer such devices, I emphasize an obvious point and segue into a basic exercise.

That dog I was working—I didn't hear him screaming in pain or fright. Did you? The collar is part of why I was able to get as much out of him so quickly. The other part is the way I used it. Consider how I teach something as basic as sit. You're used to push-on-the-butt-and-pull-on-the-collar, yes? Let me show you a kinder approach.

I borrow another untrained dog and demonstrate my method of teaching "Sit." Then I cover my techniques for teaching "Heel" and "Stay." In minutes the second dog is also responding as well as the first and the group is tuning in.

I demonstrate how I teach other basics, such as lie down, come to me, the finish and so forth. After covering any technique, I ask the student whose dog I used for illustration to work the animal. Only after the owner begins to get the same result do we progress to another topic.

A type of question that can pop up goes like this: "That first dog you worked— why didn't you correct him for leaning against you?"

He didn't know it was wrong. I correct only for out-and-out resistance: "I know what you want and I won't do it!" Besides, had I bumped the dog away when all he was trying to do was send me affection, he could have felt rejected. Later, once the animal knows some things, I'd deal with wanting my own space, but not yet. It's too soon. Teach approximates, then polish. And never put spirit at risk.

IT'S PARTLY WHY YOU GO

Regardless of the students' training proficiency there are certain concepts you should address. These areas comprise, in a nutshell, your training philosophy. Yes, you're going to cover a good many of training's mechanics, perhaps starting with such essentials as how to hold a leash. But along with teaching technical aspects you need to explain the hows and whys of training as you view them. To do otherwise is to dispense minutiae without providing an overview, a framework upon which students may pull details into a coherent whole.

DISTRACTION CONDITIONING

After dealing with how to teach various basics we progress to distraction proofing. Seminar students are often competition-oriented and, as anyone who's ever competed knows all too well, the difficulty is not in teaching a dog the routines, it's getting her to perform despite nearby goings-on.

We've all seen dogs whose obedience was okay when in the back yard. But get that animal into a ring or trial-field setting and the results can differ greatly. Improper, inadequate conditioning sinks many an outing. Just as when teaching pooch a given exercise you also must teach her that she must do it, you have to show the critter that part of your commands means that she must tune out her environment and respond only to you, not to what's happening around her. The way to do that is by showing the dog over time that she can always trust you, that you'll never put her in a situation she can't handle.

At this point I set up distraction after distraction for those dogs who are ready to handle them. I have the owners work their pets nearby while I coach the students about communicating the message that the animals must listen only to number one.

Now, let me give you some advice that students have told me was worth their seminar fee alone: Keep your distractions realistic and reasonable. Let me tell you what I mean.

I remember one training group that stay-conditioned dogs by placing them on stays and then running large, radio-controlled model cars at them. Any dog who moved got the daylights knocked out of him.

After a few "Damned idiots!" from the group, I continue.

Sure, that's not just foolishness, it's cruelty. A realistic approach would have people talking and walking back and forth behind the animals, someone dropping a lawn chair nearby, a tennis ball tossed into the show area. In terms of AKC rings, those are realistic, reasonable distractions. They're part of what can happen at a dog show.

But radio-controlled cars? Firecrackers going off a few feet from the dogs? Such distractions aren't just unrealistic, they're unreasonable. If some fool should drop firecrackers near my dog—not that I've ever seen it happen—I'd want the animal to move. That's just good sense on the dog's part. To remain in place could cause serious injury.

Realistic and reasonable—those are the keys to distraction work. Questions?

I give the group a few moments to digest what's been said.

Now, there's a related element to the "realistic and reasonable" notion: Distractions should be natural in their presentation. Consider this example.

Let's say a dog has a penchant for tennis balls. This is good because you can capitalize on his attraction toward the toys during drive work, which we'll get into in a little while. But let's say the dog has never been shown that heeling is heeling, regardless of the presence or absence of tennis balls.

So one day the trainer commands "Stay" and places tennis balls around the training area. The dog sees that after each placement the trainer stares at him. The trainer returns to the dog, commands "Heel" and sees that while the animal is heeling alright, he's nervous, salivating, panting.

What's the problem here?

I give everyone a few minutes to express ideas. If no one nails the one I'm after, I explain.

Okay, two things can go wrong with this technique. First, when the trainer looks at the dog, no message is received. The dog senses that the trainer is trying to say something about the tennis balls but the animal can have no idea what it is. The dog worries he's missed something and this makes him nervous. He knows that before when he's missed signals he's received force. Now the animal is trying to avoid pressure but has no idea how because he doesn't know what to expect or what to do. He might even think he's supposed to grab one of the toys.

That can lead to a second pitfall. Should the dog try to grab a ball during heeling he'll be corrected. That is, he'll be punished for the trainer's faulty communication.

A better ploy would be scattering the toys before bringing pooch to the area. Then they can be used as distractions but without the added mental burden that can result from placing them in the dog's presence.

Along with distraction conditioning, the group and I spend time on conceptual enhancements, many of which are outlined in the first chapter of *Advanced Obedience—Easier Than You Think*.

COMPULSION AND DRIVE

In essential terms, compulsion is force: Physical, verbal or both. It's used to make a dog behave a certain way. In my training system the pinch collar symbolizes compulsion.

Drive training capitalizes upon canine instincts toward stimuli to which he is drawn. It is used to "make" a dog do things he could not be made to do otherwise, such as to enjoy obedience. A single object or concept equatable with drive is less easily identified. Frisbees, tennis balls and other toys generally serve more of a play function than as an aid to drive training. This is because play can be difficult to link with obedience without a loss of reliability.

A training technique of my own devising, which I call the *Guard Game,* fills this gap through the canine mind-set induced by the activity and the spillover effect it has on a dog's perception of working. The game is to drive as the collar is to compulsion. It sates a host of powerful drives: Prey, retrieve, play, dominance and—to an extent—fighting. The technique establishes rock-solid control that endures even when leash and collar aren't in use.

Teaching the guard game and its applications are outlined in *Advanced Obedience—Easier Than You Think*. The game's effect on training is it teaches a dog to concentrate for a prolonged period, tuning out the rest of the world in the process.

I teach the guard game at all seminars. Simply put, it's a showstopper. Most students quickly grasp the game's implications and potential usefulness. As one seminar student stated years ago, "This is what's been missing from my training program."

ADVANCED TRAINING, COMPETITION AND PROBLEM SOLVING

From the perspective of most seminar students, these three areas are so intertwined as to be inseparable. For example, a dog walks rather than leaps over a broad jump. The broad jump is *advanced training* required in AKC Open *competition,* and when a dog walks across the hurdle, the trainer has to do some *problem solving.*

I delay foraging into any of these areas until I've covered the basics. Why? For the same reason I first work with novice dogs: So inexperienced students can keep up with the program.

For instance, my approach to teaching the retrieve is to present it not as new and distinct but as an offshoot of Companion Obedience's sit-stay and recall. With a seasoned trainer I can briefly explain technique adaptations and he or she can follow the outline. Many novices, however, unfamiliar with subtler conceptual aspects of sit-stay and recall training, would have no frame of reference for understanding extensions of those lessons.

Another determinant to successfully addressing advanced work, competition and problem solving is to restrict discussion in those areas to the needs of students and their dogs. That may seem obvious but I've watched instructors spend hours on exercises at which the handlers and dogs were more than proficient, and on work that was beyond all present. I've also seen problems solved irrespective of the fact that they didn't exist, except in the instructor's mind. Time can be an ally or an enemy in seminar teaching. The key is in how it's used.

"ADVANCED" STUDENTS

A problem instructors frequently encounter goes like this. Clinic organizers advise you'll be working with highly advanced trainers and dogs. Soon after the workshop begins you realize the animals' foundational training is riddled with gaps—big ones. This now leaves you a total quandary, "Now what?"

You don't want to throw cold water on anyone's parade, yet you have an obligation to deal in reality. Your first order of business has to be helping all participants shore up the basics. That is, after all, why they enrolled. To do otherwise is to attempt to build on a foundation of sand.

Still, how to bring folks back to earth in gentle fashion? My approach is to ask each owner to work his or her pet on basics while the group and I critique. The obvious is soon exemplified: Training to date has not had the desired effect. Involving the group takes the onus off you while establishing starting points from which to progress.

PARTAKE NOT

Here's another mine field you may have to negotiate. During a break you find yourself chatting with several students. Someone makes disparaging comments about a local or regional trainer or training group. Other folks begin to share in the sentiments.

Now, the observations may be justified. The trainer or club being castigated may be more than deserving. Heaven knows there is no shortage of ignorance and incompetence in the realm of dog training. But if I may offer a bit of advice: Stay out of it. Don't be drawn in. Don't stray past plain-vanilla ripostes.

Why? Because while you may think you're making friends by appearing sympathetic, your listeners may later worry, "I wonder what he's saying about us." That's risk number one. The second is—and I assure you it will happen—your observations will be misquoted and will very probably find their way to the group that was being hammered. Not only might those folks conclude that you're an irresponsible gossip, you can forget about ever doing a seminar for them.

If someone tries to pin you down—"Well, what do you think of all this?"—your best response, even to tales of maltreatment and abuse, is akin to, "Maybe I'll meet those people someday."

THE PROPHET SYNDROME

During a seminar it may happen that your solution to a training problem will be identical to that repeatedly suggested by a local instructor. But—and here's the interesting part—even though the latter's advice was ignored, your counsel may be seen as divinely inspired.

Why? There are several reasons but the primary one is that, as you are from out of the area, it's a certainty you must know more than any local teacher. Sure, that's fuzzy reasoning, but people think like that. It's a heck of an insight into the often-strange dips of human nature.

This harkens to the theme, "Responsibility" from chapter 5, "Teaching Guidelines." Though you're part of the scenery when you're home, you're an authority when you're on the road. There's an old proverb about a prophet having no honor in his own country. Right or wrong, the reality is that seminar students may attach undue weight to your pronouncements.

For clinic instructors this can be a trap. Anyone is at least somewhat susceptible to ego-stroking, and being cast as a guru can sometimes cause a person to take him- or herself too seriously. When that happens, the very talents that caused the sponsoring group to engage an instructor's services can be dulled as a result of the individual's lost perspective. True, you're an expert in your field, else you would not have been invited, but bear in mind that first you are a guest.

ABERRATIONS

Among students who attend seminars is a troubled minority. They don't go to learn anything, but to prove to themselves—and to anyone who will listen—that they know more than the instructor. Often devotees of harsh training methods, it is these types whom Louis "Satchmo" Armstrong had in mind when he observed, "There are some people that if they don't know, you can't tell 'em." Because they haven't figured out that status, power and control are illusions, these lock steppers are driven by appetites for each that approach monomania. As existence for them is like a drawn bow, they radiate all the joie de vivre of an impacted wisdom tooth. Living through their dogs, taking bows for the animals' triumphs while ducking responsibility for training's miscues, theirs is perhaps the cruelest addiction of all, pride and vanity being the beguilers they are.

If you've been in the business awhile you've encountered these unhappy souls. If you're new to the circuit, be aware. These people know what they know, and they perceive change, especially change not originating with them, as threatening unto their fiefdoms. Their security derives from a need to feel superior, and to inflate themselves they attempt to belittle others.

Truly professional trainers/teachers are comfortable with themselves and with their ways of doing things. They deal from acceptance, not unresolved anger. As dogs work best when in sync with their handlers, no dog can be content around someone who is discontented with himself. Most dog people are caring folks drawn to canine contact for all the right reasons. Fame and fortune are the guiding stars for others, however, and these people are often accorded rank only because their methods are strikingly counter to what seems reasonable. That, and such luminaries are quite adept at wielding psychological battering rams against people and dogs alike.

Though I've yet to discover a universal method for defusing fanaticism, I can tell you that neither appeasement nor inflexibility are likely to change anything. Better allies are patience, deflection and a sense of humor. These approaches are infinitely preferable to tacit approval or, "Because I said so, dammit!"

What you must not do is let "in-your-face" challenges to your authority get to you. These people are present only because they don't know where else to be. Don't take absurdity seriously, and "Avoid loud and aggressive persons; they are vexations to the spirit."[2] Simply accept the truisms that new ideas can further unsettle those who define themselves from without, and that no one has the power to change anyone else. Our obligation is to plant seeds, not to take responsibility for their germination.

REFLECTION

There's a story told by the American Indians, which goes that the Great Spirit decided to divide the worlds of animals and man. So He gathered all the living beings on a great plain and drew a line in the dirt. On one side of the line stood man, on the other side stood all the animals; and that line began to open up into a great chasm, and at the last moment, before it became unbreachable, dog leapt over and stood by man.

—ROGER A. CARAS IN *Dogs,*
FROM TURNER ORIGINAL PRODUCTIONS

---

[2]From *Desiderata,* by Max Erhmann.

Chapter 16

IMPAIRED OWNERS

I often saw them during my morning trek to school. The man was short, slender and white-haired; he walked with a limp and his right arm was paralyzed. His dog was a Great Pyrenees, proud, alert and—though I didn't know the word then—majestic. I knew many people who had dogs but something special hummed between these two, something an adult might miss but a third-grader couldn't. In a phrase, they were tuned to the same frequency. That, and the man had trained his dog well. Even amid busy morning traffic, Barney never skipped a beat, always staying right next to Mr. Jamison. Truly a gentle man, he may have owned a leash but I never saw him use one.

One morning Barney wasn't there. "He's at the vet's," Mr. Jamison told me, "Some sort of bug, but he'll be okay."

Later that day I realized it was the first time I ever saw Mr. Jamison using a cane. He had it the next day, too, and for a few days afterward, but that didn't say much to me at the time. I was concerned about Barney; and besides, a cane was something old people used sometimes.

A week or so later Barney was back. His tail at full wag, he washed my face as I ran my hands through the huge, gentle animal's profuse coat. I didn't notice until the next morning that Mr. Jamison no longer had a cane, and that he'd not had it the day before. I'd been around dogs since my earliest memories, and had always felt something of an affinity with them, but the day I began to home in on *Canis familiaris* took place years later during my teens when I realized that after Barney returned to Mr. Jamison, I never saw him use a cane again.

Now, what does this story say to you? Does it suggest the psychological and emotional lift a good dog can provide to a physically impaired person? I imagine it may, but a good dog can do that for nearly anyone, disabled or not. During what must have been a slow time, scientists have gotten around to documenting what most of us have known all along: Pets are good for people.

This tale's significance is something of a sleeper. Consider again, "The man was short, slender, white-haired, walked with a limp, and his right arm was paralyzed." Then add, "Barney never skipped a beat, always staying right next to Mr. Jamison, who may have owned a leash but I never saw him use one."

A dog off-leash, amid pedestrian and vehicular traffic (and the occasional stray dog or cat), wearing just a leather collar—that's more than many able-bodied trainers ever accomplish. It's also where you and I come in. You see, Obedience classes were virtually unheard of in the town where and when I grew up. Mr. Jamison once told me, when I commented on how well-mannered Barney was, "There are easier things than training a dog when you've never done it before, especially with Barney nearly as big as I am, and me with this damn gimp arm." (Mr. Jamison didn't mention it, but he had a balance problem, too.) He had studied training books, also few in number in those days, at the library, and had achieved impressive results, disabilities notwithstanding. But I think Mr. Jamison would have agreed that training his (truly great) Pyr would have been much easier with the help of someone versed in the art. As I said, that's where you and I enter the picture.

WHAT DOES IMPAIRED MEAN?

The first thing to acknowledge is you've been working with disabled folks right along, assuming you've been teaching classes for any length of time. True, you may yet to have enrolled a wheelchair user or someone on crutches, but has there not been a student who needed glasses for more than just reading, or wore a hearing aid? Perhaps you have had a student that was a bit slow of mind or so uneducated that he or she may not have understood your every word, or was unable to read your class handouts?

Have you not enrolled someone so emotionally frail that tiny problems were seen as huge? Was there never a student in any of your classes so unable to feel that canine messages of affection and trust just didn't penetrate?

How about a person so overweight that the individual was hesitant to bend over, fearful that he or she might fall and not be able to get back up? Surely you have enrolled senior citizens whose reaction time, dexterity and strength has faded?

"When a second-week dog heels on a loose leash this well,
who needs crutches?" said the owner. She has a point.

What of folks with chronic back or knee problems, or those who have a phobia about groups of people, even small ones? I've had more than one such student, and others who were frightened to be near (pick one): Dobermans, Rottweilers, German Shepherds—even Cockers; it's a long list. As you can see, in addition to those who must rely on mechanical devices, the criteria for being disabled can be extensive, and I imagine you could expand the foregoing.

All this begs the question, Are some people too disabled to train a dog in a public Obedience class? Answer: Sure, though we're talking extremes now. If a person can "get around," he or she probably can train a dog. As a friend of mine, a wheelchair user, once commented, "The only limits on training your pet are the ones you place on yourself."

THE RIGHT DOG

That last paragraph intersects a second concept. A barrier that no one should try to circumvent is that of owning more dog than he or she can handle. Thus, a primary service that instructors can offer is advising folks on how to select the right dog. We seldom have this opportunity, as most callers already own a dog. Every so often, however, you may be contacted by an impaired person, or the relative of one, seeking advice about what type of dog might be a good companion. Size and temperament are two primary considerations. Size in the sense that—just as someone who uses crutches may be overmatched by an Irish Wolfhound—a wheelchair user may not be able to reach a Miniature Pinscher. The dog's temperament should be stable, even and steady. The animal should be drawn to human companionship and should show no signs of independent character or being aggressive toward other dogs.

Some might consider that a German Shepherd is too much dog for a wheelchair user. Owner Lynn Dickey didn't think so, and Duchess proved her right.

GENERALITIES

Essential to working with handicapped students is realizing that they are seldom as disadvantaged as the average person might believe. They're far from helpless, rank high in courage and resourcefulness, and generally (and properly) resent attempts to treat them as different. Look, I can walk and run but a wheelchair user can't. A friend of mine can effortlessly toss about a 100-pound bale of hay but I can barely move one. Does that make any of us different? Certainly not. Not in spirit, where that kind of thing counts. We just have different abilities, different limitations.

So long as a student can teach pooch the obedience desired, treat the individual like anyone else, because—in terms of ability to train a dog—he or she is like anyone else. As a dear friend once put it, "He's a person with a disability, not a disabled person." Sure, your expectations may have to be adjusted a bit: When I tell a class practicing heeling, "Run," I don't expect someone who uses a walker to comply. But I do expect a deaf person to, or one who has emotional problems or is a slow learner.

In the proverbial nutshell, my approach to teaching physically disadvantaged students is to show them how to perform a given action, not to show them how they're limited. They know their limitations better than I ever could, and surely don't need an outsider to point them out.

SPECIFICS

For safety reasons alone, I require that all blind or deaf students be accompanied at class by a friend of theirs. Not only might a blind or deaf person not sense an aggressive dog's approach, the risk of other types of accidents could be higher. In terms of learning, the assistance of a friend at a dog-obedience class is a great aid to a blind or deaf individual. True, many deaf people are excellent lip readers, but not all are. Besides, that skill is useful only if the instructor is facing that particular student at all times, which isn't always possible in a class setting.

The buddy-system concept is also mandatory in my classes for manual-wheelchair users who are new to training or who are training novice dogs. Again, this is for safety reasons, though in a different vein. As two hands are required to propel the chair, leash management is not only difficult, a lead can easily become enmeshed in a wheel. Also, when classes are held on lawns, wheelchair operation takes considerable effort. The ground's surface appears smooth but in reality is dotted with myriad bumps and dips. This isn't to say that you shouldn't include impaired students in on-the-green classes, but that if you also offer sessions on a gym floor, for instance, the student might have an easier time indoors.

A serious training problem for cane, crutch or walker users can be maintaining balance. A large dog bumping the owner, or a smaller animal getting underfoot, can result in a fall. The problem is compounded by the fact that the handler's devices cause slow movement that leads to canine inattention. Though this is understandable in dog terms—the owner not moving fast enough to hold the animal's interest—loss of focus is equally unacceptable. I've found that repetitive about turns made in place to the right are helpful toward a solution, especially during initial stages of teaching heeling. They cause the dog to cover more ground than he would doing straight-line heeling, and thus tend to keep him more alert.

Another difficulty faced by cane, crutch or walker users, and folks who are extremely overweight or have back or knee problems, is getting onto the ground to teach "Platz." I recommend these people have a friend show the dog the exercise, taking over with leash-on-pole equipment once the animal understands the command. For students who are able to get down next to pooch, but who would have difficulty doing so repeatedly, I suggest that once they are on the ground, they remain there. After the dog is lying down, the handler should move him from the Platz position by slight knee movement and, if needed, a gentle tug on the collar. The dog will rise, move a few inches, be told "Sit," and can then be shown "Platz" again.

EXTRA EQUIPMENT

Training can be made easier for wheelchair or scooter[1] users and their pets by affixing a short strip of leash and snap to the end of a three- to four-foot length of wooden doweling. The pole should be of sufficient diameter that it would be unlikely to break when used to exert pressure. The amount of leash available can be varied by attaching it via a series of eye-hooks screwed into the doweling, allowing the lead to slip back and forth. Most users, however, find that a variable length of lead, though sometimes useful, tends to make for difficult handling. Thus, I pay out the amount of leash that seems appropriate and use duct tape to attach the balance to the doweling, thereby making constant the length of the lead protruding from the staff. The snap of a second lead attached to the doweling's end can facilitate teaching "Platz!" In either configuration, a device such as this can not only prevent a lead from fouling in wheelchair or scooter wheels, the leverage it affords can simplify teaching such obedience functions as heeling and sit.

PSYCHOLOGICALLY IMPAIRED STUDENTS

When working with mentally slow or retarded people, breaking lessons into steps is vital. I know: That principle is elucidated in chapter 5, "Teaching Guidelines." But I restate it here to accent its importance for working with those who have learning difficulties. Years ago a student who was a child trapped in an adult's body had trouble teaching "Sit." She couldn't remember the sequence. So I told her, "Say 'Sit,' make pooch sit, say 'Good sit' and pet your dog. Three steps, Karen, three." Her dog soon learned to sit. The key was in compartmentalizing the steps and—very important—in telling Karen how many elements were involved. I remember the first time she made the connection: She said "Sit," pushed her dog into position, said "Good sit" and petted him. Karen thought for a few seconds, then excitedly looked at me with a million-dollar smile and said, "Three! That's three!"[2]

---

[1] A manual wheelchair is not the same as a motorized chair, and neither is the same as a scooter. If you are unfamiliar with these devices, I suggest you contact medical personnel for further information.

[2] Petting could be construed as a fourth step, and for some students may have to be identified as such.

Repetition is a second fundamental for working with a slow learner. After Karen spoke to me I told her, "You did good, Karen. Real good. Let's do it again." And again, and again. As I've written earlier, once you're on a roll, stay with it.

Less than emotionally stable students sometimes tend to panic. I've seen folks become tearful when their pets didn't perform correctly, and when they did. My general response is to treat the person as though nothing unusual is happening, as though they are acting "normally" (whatever that is), in the hope that the attitude will be adopted.

Variations on "Calm down" tend to be less effective, as many psychologically impaired persons have already heard them too often throughout their lives. Telling someone how to feel doesn't work; at best it's a temporary Band-Aid. While I can't give you a one-size-fits-all solution for dealing with folks whose emotional boat is easily rocked, I do suggest that you can't allow yourself to get caught up in the moment. That's not to say an answer lies in impersonality, in mechanical sterility. Coldness, like colds, is contagious, and can cause students to lock up.

ADDITIONAL TRAINING

As stated in the Preface, *Teaching Obedience Classes and Seminars* is not a training manual. Hence, an area I've left untouched is training techniques per se. Teachers should realize, however, that a few after-class minutes spent with a handicapped person, showing the individual how to teach his or her pet a few extras, can be a boon for the student. Heeling, sits, stays and so forth are all very useful, no question, but ask a wheelchair user if he or she also would like to teach pooch to pick up and return a dropped object (or to jump into his or her lap), and you may see some eyes light up.

COMPETITION

Question: Should an impaired owner show his or her dog in Obedience competition?

Answer: If the owner wishes to and the dog is up to it, why not?

There are, however, some problem areas. Consider the following Recall excerpt from the AKC *Obedience Regulations* (amended to January 1, 1994), page 29: "The dog must . . . sit straight, centered immediately in front of the handler's feet, close enough that the handler could readily touch its [sic] head without moving either foot or having to stretch forward." A dog, especially a small one, centered immediately in front of a scooter user's feet would be too far away for the handler to reach without "having to stretch forward."

Another question is, How can a walker user respond to the "Fast" directive during heeling? Also, for many cane, crutch or walker users, "walk briskly and in a natural manner"[3] is an oxymoron. I could cite other incongruities, not the least of which relates to defining the Heel Position, but I imagine you get the point.

Nancy West and her Cocker Spaniel, Jake, CDX, TDI, after a successful outing.

True, Section 14—Disabled Handlers, provides, "Judges may modify the specific requirements of these Regulations for handlers to the extent necessary to permit disabled handlers to compete."[4] Now, most judges are like you and me, in the sense that they welcome all entrants and deal with atypical situations gracefully. However, a minority haven't had an original thought since personally experiencing the dawn of reason. They seem to validate the *Peter Principle*.[5] Consider this example.

---

[3]Ibid, p. 27.

[4]Ibid, p. 19.

[5]The *Peter Principle* holds that a failing of many organizations is that numerous of its membership eventually ascend to their own levels of incompetence.

The UD hopeful was a scooter user. She sought the opinions of two judges about the Scent Discrimination rule that requires the exhibitor to "turn in place"[6] to face the articles after they've been placed. As she explained to the judges, a scooter cannot be turned in place; the machine necessitates additional room to execute a 180-degree turn.

No problem, right? Just have the handler move forward and to the left, then turn back to the right until she arrives at the starting position. Or direct her to move forward, backup to the left, and turn right until she and pooch are facing the articles. The judges advised the lady that either of these solutions, in addition to others discussed, would not be acceptable, that in effect if she could not turn in place, she was out of luck. Like I said about original thoughts and the dawn of reason.

Anyone with enough sense to differentiate a dog from a cat three times out of four also should be able to see that a scooter cannot "turn in place." Granted, the rule reads as the rule reads but what does it mean? Is the inference that someone using a machine requiring room to make an about-turn is not permitted to compete? I can't believe that, but perhaps some learned judges apparently forgot the spirit of the Scent Discrimination rule's opening paragraph: "The *principal* (italics by author) features of these exercises are the selection of the handler's article from among the other articles by scent alone, and the prompt delivery of the right article to the handler."[7]

My points here are twofold. Competitors should realize that not every judge suffers under a burden of common sense; and the AKC should reword certain of its rules so that judges of limited vision don't have to give themselves a headache by trying to think.

SHOULD AN IMPAIRED INDIVIDUAL . . .

Teach Obedience classes? I know some who do. In the interests of safety, they restrict their enrollments to dogs they or assistants can "physically overpower should the need arise," but I offer that advice to all instructors.[8] As indicated, helpers may be needed, depending upon the teacher's disability; but so long as

---

[6]Ibid, p. 42.

[7]AKC *Obedience Regulations,* amended to January 1, 1994, p. 41.

[8]See the section entitled, "Physical Limitations," in chapter 3, "Before Your Phone Rings."

he or she can run safe classes, and can communicate and demonstrate that which students need to know, impaired is a moot point.

SEMANTICS AND SENSITIVITY

You may encounter people who take offense at certain terms, *disabled, disadvantaged, handicapped* and *impaired* among them. While it's true that some folks bluster no matter how they're referred to, one way to avoid being unaware of the week's politically correct term for any group is to avoid using such labels. When watching students train, all an instructor need differentiate are the teams that are doing okay versus those who need assistance. Further categorization of owners experiencing difficulty could be nothing more than an attempt to fix blame rather than fix the problem.

CLOSURE

This is one of those chapters that could be expanded into a book. The difficulty in composing it is in deciding what areas to touch on, which ones to scrutinize, and which ones to ignore. Still, whether we're discussing a chapter or a book or a footnote on the subject of human impairments, the following gentle elegance offers keen insight.

REFLECTION

For perhaps, if the truth were known, we're all a little blind, a little deaf, a little handicapped, a little lonely, a little less than perfect. And if we can learn to appreciate and utilize the dog's full potentials, we will, together, make it in this life on earth.

—CHARLOTTE SCHWARTZ,
FRIEND TO FRIEND—DOGS THAT HELP MANKIND

Chapter 17

PROBLEMS AND SOLUTIONS

Not everything occurs in a nice, neat, ordered fashion in the Obedience class instruction business (nor in any other business that I know). This chapter covers oddball matters, the likes of which have a way of popping up. While addressing every conceivable problem isn't possible, sufficient generalities are provided to give you a sense of how to manage with similar difficulties.

Problem: Though you require full payment at enrollment, a student says, "I forgot my checkbook at home. Can I pay next week?"

Solution: Answer, "Sure," and record the amount owed in a memo to yourself. To demand that the student return home to fetch her checkbook could result in your not seeing her again and your name and policies being vilified among her friends.

Problem: A student's check bounces.

Solution: If the person is enrolled in your local classes, contact him and request the check be replaced with cash. If the individual is enrolled for a seminar, contact the sponsors and ask them to intercede on your behalf.

As a corollary, become familiar with credit practices and legal remedies in your area. Learning what your options are makes good sense for any professional.

Problem: A small dog is at full yip, making hearing difficult for everyone. The animal is nervous, not aggressive.

Solution: Ask the owner to pick up and hold the critter for awhile. Smaller dogs do most of such carrying on and often can be settled with a little reassurance rather than harshness.

Problem: A student arrives with a sick dog.

Solution: This pertains to local classes and seminars: The student may stay, the dog may not. Get that animal out of there, forthwith.

Problem: An owner wants to attend with a bitch in heat.

Solution: Nope. The bitch's presence is not just too hard on the other animals, it's too stressful for her. Tell the owner you'll be glad to call when your next series starts, when the bitch may also be out of season.

Problem: A caller wishes to enroll a pregnant animal.

Solution: Advise that the bitch has enough to deal with for now, and to delay training until the pups are weaned and have been started on their vaccinations. Also warn the caller that the bitch could easily pick up a bug at class and infect the unborn litter.

Problem: A student informs you that, for whatever reason, he or she refuses to have pooch vaccinated.

Solution: I've run into this one a few times, the owners' unwillingness often being based on religious convictions. In each instance I've listened to what they had to say, then expressed my regret at being unable to enroll them. You cannot sanction exposure of dogs to an unvaccinated animal, or vice versa.

Problem: One type of question students ask relates to health.

"My dog has a lump. Would you look at it?"

"Sometimes my dog throws up. What's that mean?"

"My dog acts like one of his legs hurts. Any ideas?"

Solution: My answer for those questions and others like them is the same: "Contact your vet." Sure, I may suspect what the trouble is and what, if anything, to do about it. But I'm a trainer/instructor, not a veterinarian, and it may be that my well-intentioned advice could result in disaster. Just as veterinarians should direct training questions to trainers, canine medical issues should be addressed by qualified professionals.

Problem: Another kind of question instructors must field relates to problem behaviors.

"What can I do about my dog digging holes in the yard?"

"How do I stop my dog from chasing cars?"

"What can I do about my dog getting into the garbage?"

And so on. If you've taught classes for any length of time, you've been asked about these problems and many others like them. If you're new to the business, prepare yourself.

Solution: As a general rule I table such questions should they arise at a first-week class. While common problems like jumping on the owner can be quickly resolved, undesirable behaviors such as excessive barking and submissive urination are better delayed until the dog knows a few basic commands and the owner has established a communication framework from which to operate.

Problem: A student suggests you should provide a community water bucket for class dogs.

Solution: Don't do it. Owners may bring water and bowls for their dogs, of course, but using a common water source for all comers is an excellent way to transmit disease.

Problem: A dog is already reliable to a command other than the one you recommend for a given exercise.

Solution: Much wisdom resides in the aphorism, "If it ain't broke, don't fix it." If you prefer "Platz" for commanding a dog to lie down, for instance, and an owner has taught "Down," leave well enough alone. The student may elect to change the command but should not be pressured into making that choice.

Problem: These next three are a series. First, a student wishes to use a vocabulary of commands other than those you suggest.

Solution: Fine.

Problem: An owner doesn't care to teach the finish and prefers right-side heeling.

Solution: Fine.

Problem: A student with a tough dog adamantly refuses even to try a pinch collar.

Solution: Not fine. Refund the individual's money and suggest he or she try another trainer.

My point here is one of establishing lines you won't cross. While using different commands and not teaching peripheral exercises won't hurt a dog, the wrong equipment can. A choker on an animal having low touch sensitivity can cause permanent injury.

Problem: A caller wishes to train a handicapped dog.

Solution: Why not? I've worked with owners of blind animals, deaf ones, dogs who were permanently lame and some who'd lost a leg. You may have to alter a requirement or two, and you may have to modify your training techniques; but so long as the owner believes in his or her pet, go for it.

Should the subject of AKC competition arise, however, be sure the student knows that a dog who is blind, deaf, lame or who is bandaged cannot be shown.

Problem: A student tells you that it will be impossible to follow the one-trainer rule, that scheduling difficulties necessitate someone else bringing pooch to class once or twice.

Solution: I recommend going along with this. As a trainer you know that dogs generally learn easier from one person than from several. As an instructor you'll find that "one dog, one trainer" is not always possible and that a dog is better trained by more than one person than trained by no one.

Problem: A student tells you he or she will have to miss a session.

Solution: Catch up the student privately if your schedules permit, or suggest the individual arrive early at the subsequent class for a brief, make-up lesson.

Problem: A student's pet becomes ill (or the student does) and, adhering to your rule of not bringing a sick dog to class, they miss two consecutive lessons.

Solution: Offer to enroll the person in your next series at no further charge. Too much has been missed to try and catch the team up with the rest of the class. True, it's not your fault someone became ill but it's not the student's either.

Problem: For reasons other than illness a student is unable to finish a class series.

Solution: Offer to include the person in a subsequent series at no further charge. You are under no obligation to refund any portion of your fee, however, as you did hold space for the team.

Problem: A student who missed a class but who was able to make up the work wants to know if he or she will receive a diploma.

Solution: "Of course, you will."

Problem: A first-class no-show whom you were unable to contact after the initial session arrives at your second meeting.

Solution: This one's a judgement call. An exceptionally trainable dog owned by a motivated, teachable person may be able to catch up. Generally, however, the interests of all concerned are better served by suggesting the owner wait until your next series.

Problem: A caller advises that his or her dog is super aggressive.

Solution: Work privately with the student if you wish, or turn down the business. It's immoral (not to mention unethical) to expose people and their pets to a known threat case. Further, should such a dog bite someone or injure a dog at class, you could be open for any number of legal difficulties.

Problem: Though as rare as highly aggressive dogs, students can be hostile too. You may encounter some who continually make comments akin to, "That's certainly not how we did it in another class I took!" Such people aren't just distractive but disruptive and tend to resist most everything you say.

Solution: Realizing that some folks would argue with a signpost, have a private word with the student and try to find out what the problem is. There's no need for excoriation but if you can't reconcile the difficulty, point out the options: The person can either lighten up or hit the road. You're there to teach according to your principles, not to engage in endless debates with uninformed, uninformable antagonists.

Problem: A student physically or verbally abuses his or her pet. When confronted, you're informed that such methods are proper, according to so-and-so's book.

Solution: Clarify that this is your class, not so-and-so's, and that you won't tolerate abuse of a helpless animal.

Problem: A student brings youngsters to class. Despite your expressed wishes, the children do not, "remain quietly in one place," but continually run about the training area and disrupt the proceedings.

Solution: Your job is to teach people how to train dogs, not discipline children. Remind the parent that the kids must accede to the "Stay" command or you'll be unable to allow their presence.

Problem: Soon after a first-week class you hear from someone who wants to enroll but doesn't wish to wait until your next series.

Solution: If you're so inclined and have room in a class, meet privately with the individual and get him or her caught up for the current series.

Problem: At a first-week class composed of your maximum number of enrollments, you discover that a student has brought a friend who also wishes to sign up.

Solution: Enroll the unanticipated student and reconcile yourself to teaching a slightly larger number than you prefer. If several unexpected students show up, split the class into two or more groups.

Problem: In several instances I've suggested that you meet individually with a student. That can raise the question, "Do I charge additionally for the private session?"

Solution: I don't. The need for personal sessions doesn't arise that often. Should a student require more than a single one-on-one lesson, then I consider assessing an additional fee.

Problem: A similar question is whether you should charge callers who ask, "Can you tell me how to housebreak my puppy?" or how to keep pooch out of the garbage, how to stop him from jumping on people, and so forth.

Solution: I not only don't charge for such advice, I ring-off by saying, "If you have any other problems, give me a call." By helping out I may wind up with a student. Refusal or asking for the owner's VISA card number would make that far less likely.

Problem: After several weeks of observing, an apprentice wishes to teach a session or a series.

Solution: Not a good idea. Though I wouldn't dismiss the request reflex-ively—there can always be exceptions to any rule—your students have enrolled to learn about training from you, not from someone who is learning about teach-ing.

That's the moral argument. There are also legal considerations. Should some-thing "go wrong": Injury to a dog, a bitten student—it's a long list of possibili-ties—you could find yourself in a court of law (i.e., a roomful of professional second-guessers), defending yourself over why you allowed someone without experience to handle a situation requiring the attention of an experienced pro-fessional.

Problem: A student has out-of-town visitors and wishes to bring them to class.

Solution: Sure, but afford yourself a measure of legal protection by having each adult visitor sign your Agreement (see chapter 2, "Simplicity").

Problem: At what point should you cancel due to inclement weather?

Solution: A light rain shower or brief snow flurries are not sufficient reason to call off a regularly scheduled class, but hazardous roads are. Also, extreme temperatures and/or high winds may necessitate cancellation if you hold classes outdoors.

Problem: What about canceling for various holidays?

Solution: I cancel for New Year's Day, Thanksgiving and Christmas. For Easter, Memorial Day, the Fourth of July and Labor Day I put cancellation to a vote of the students. If the group wishes not to go ahead with a session, I abide by the collective decision. However, I would not initiate a series on any of the fore-going legal holidays.

When canceling for a holiday, be sure to announce the fact at the preceding class; don't presume the students will know not to show up. Similarly, it's wise to remind everyone, "Remember: Next weekend daylight saving time changes to standard time (or vice-versa) but we'll still meet at the same scheduled hour." Failure to clarify this point can have students arriving at the wrong time with predictable annoyance.

Problem: A few days after enrolling, a student reports that his or her dog died (or was stolen—either can happen). What should you do about this person's class fee?

Solution: Refund it. At least make the offer. No, you aren't obligated to, but to quibble over a few bucks during such a traumatic time would be heartless. A sympathy card when a student's dog has died may be appropriate and says a lot about you as a caring individual.

Problem: Same situation as before but now you're several weeks into the series.

Solution: I can't tell you where to draw this line. I seldom make refunds for any reason after completing the second class, but inflexibility in operating any business can hamstring.

Problem: A student's dog just bit you, drawing blood.

Solution: Contact an MD and do as he or she instructs. If the wound is serious, respond as you would to any critical household accident: Get to a hospital, emergency room or clinic, or call an ambulance. In any case, make certain that the dog is currently vaccinated against rabies.

Problem: A student is bitten, breaking the skin.

Solution: Recommend the same course of action given in the previous situation. I keep a first-aid kit close by, if not on display.

Problem: One dog attacks another.

Solution: Immediately intervene. Don't leave matters to owners. Yes, trying to disrupt a dogfight is risky, but in a class setting a teacher should assume such responsibilities. Like the aforementioned first-aid kit, I keep a three-foot shock-stick nearby to bring a quick halt to active hostilities.

SUMMARY

Many problems come under the heading of public relations, and as you know or will discover, easy answers can be few and far between. Taking each case individually is preferable to living by hard-and-fast rules. Applying an impersonal approach to a personal kind of business creates a needless conflict that can be reliably depended upon to cause others.

REFLECTION

Histories are more full of examples of the fidelity of dogs than of friends.

—Alexander Pope

Chapter 18

Lessons from the Best Teacher (Part IV)

With just one exception, my books conclude with a chapter on "Lessons From the Best Teacher," a collection of flashbacks about training, bonding and dogs in the general context of the subject of the particular book. The progression continues here, this time with the accent on instruction, students and their dogs.

INSIGHT

A friend of mine had discovered the three-month-old German Shepherd at an animal shelter. In dumping him there, his owners had stated he was stupid. They themselves must have possessed room-temperature IQs because . . . well, you'll see.

My friend, Adrienne, was quite taken by the pup. She bailed him out, took him home, named him Rommel and soon received a profound glimpse into canine intelligence.

Finding that housebreaking at Rommel's former home had entailed paper-training, Adrienne taught him the great outdoors concept. Her preference was not just for the sake of household cleanliness, but to avoid confusing Rommel because of her practice of saving newspapers for periodic transport to a recycling center.

One evening Adrienne was luxuriating in the tub when Rommel flew into the bathroom, panicked in "that look," the one that says, "I must get outside—now!" Grabbing a towel she raced down the hallway but alas she was too late. Nature had made the demand and Rommel could only obey. But that wasn't what stopped Adrienne in her tracks. Care to guess what did?

The young Shepherd's target was a newspaper he'd pulled from the stack by the back door.

Some weeks later I recounted the incident to a trainer who is something of a theorist. He blew off the tale as a fabrication. I cautioned that Adrienne was not given to hyperbole. Unimpressed, he intoned, "Many books on canine intelligence maintain that dogs are incapable of cause-and-effect reasoning."

Fortunately, Rommel hadn't read those books. I have, and their conclusions on the reasoning abilities of *Canis familiaris* are largely incorrect. By using human intelligence as a baseline for judging the mental faculties of dogs, the authors miss the point. They compare the incomparable.

This tale is but one that supports my belief that dogs do indeed think. They do so in a manner unlike our own, yes, but they do think. The difference is that they don't think about thinking. They just do it.

Now, is every dog as bright as Rommel? No. But similar anecdotes owners have told me, together with my own observations, suggest that dogs are more cerebrally gifted than many people realize. Knowing you may encounter naysayers among your students, I've told you this story so that you could tell it to them.

A TRAINER, BUT NOT A TEACHER

In an Indiana hamlet resides an elderly gentleman who has forgotten more about dogs and training than many pros will ever know. He loves and has great respect for and rapport with dogs, can teach them just about anything, but he "ain't got much use for people." Truly, he'd starve in the diplomatic corps.

Some years ago he was sought out by several local dog owners who asked him to hold an Obedience class. His reply was terse and direct: "Thanks. Nope. Ain't interested." Those who had beseeched him held that his attitude was disgraceful, that he had an obligation toward the community. His rejoinder cannot be quoted here but know that it was brief, colorful and made up in bite what it lacked in subtlety.

Months later, when the crusty old soul told me of the incident, he commented, "My first obligation is to my own self and I'm not no teacher of people. I'm a trainer of dogs."

My purpose in sharing this account is to accent a first-chapter point: Teaching classes is not for every trainer, just as teaching seminars is not for every Obedience-class instructor, "and a wise soul respects and honors his gifts but does not push beyond his abilities."

WHAT GOES AROUND . . .

Big Red's owner had phoned about my competition-prep class. He'd stated that his two-year-old male Irish Setter was well schooled in obedience, the result of the caller having read, "a training book or two—I forget which ones." "Fact is," he continued, "with a little practice around other dogs, me and this here Irish will be getting that first AKC Obedience title out of the way."

I asked the caller if he'd ever shown a dog.

He hadn't.

"Have you ever been to a dog show?"

"Nope."

I asked if he'd trained a dog before. "Naw, but it don't seem like much of a big deal. I shouldn't have no trouble with that title."

Perhaps you'll identify with my glazed-eyed, "Un-huh" response. For those who make a living in saner ways, be advised that trainers/teachers sometimes encounter inexperienced folks who feel that a working title is as easily had as a politician's promise.

Yes, some excellent training books are available; and yes, it's possible to train a dog to competition level without further coaching. This particular gent just seemed to radiate too much bravado, especially given his notion of, "getting that first title out of the way," after which I supposed he intended to pen his first of several training books.

Anyway, the first day of class came. The man arrived and proceeded to run Big Red through his paces. A more nervously working critter I'd not seen in years. Irish Setters are typically less than stoic but this one had problems. I soon discovered that his biggest one was at the other end of the leash.

At one point Big Red broke a down-stay. I noticed he did so neither from curiosity about his new surroundings nor from an attitude of "In your ear!" disobedience. He was simply anxious. If his aspect said anything it was that he was searching for a place to hide. There quickly followed an indication of what he wanted to hide from.

The owner rushed toward Big Red, yelling all manner of language, and started to slam the Setter to the ground, having grabbed skin over the withers and hip area and lifting the dog to shoulder height. Stunned by the rapidly unfolding event, it was fortunate that I reacted in time to prevent the bug-eyed, red-faced, hyperventilating character from following through. He could have seriously injured the dog.

Once the situation had calmed I asked Big Red's owner where he'd learned such a corrective "technique." He assured me it was in a title-forgotten book he'd read. I pointed out that I'd read most of the books, had never heard of body-slamming a dog, and that regardless of what tome he'd studied, such methods would not be used at my classes. I further advised him that were he to show his paranoid partner anytime soon, neither of them would last five seconds in a ring.

Over the next several weeks, through my efforts and those of some caring students (about the dog, anyway), the man began to put his ego on hold. Finally, Big Red himself drove the message home. During a stand for exam, after the owner had returned to the heel position, the Irish lifted a leg on him. Impressively so. Normally I can maintain my composure but I confess it was the best thigh-slapper I'd had in months.

"Awright, just what the hell does *that* mean?" the shocked owner screamed at me. Between tearful, breathless, gut-grabbing guffaws, I rhetorically replied, "What do you think it means?"

In truth I'd witnessed the phenomenon before and suspected that it had as much to do with marking as with disdain. In any case the event signified a turning point. The guy settled over the next few weeks, his praise became more sincere and Big Red began to trust him. Such is the humbling, forgiving nature of these loyal creatures.

The points? First, dogs will often endure fierce human mistreatment without developing a grudge.[1] The sad truth is abused animals often come to feel there must be an inherent fault within themselves, else the maltreatment would not occur.

---

[1] See Learned-helplessness syndrome in the Glossary.

Second, sometimes you have to let the dog teach the owner. Impatience urged me more than once to run this bird down the road, but while doing so would have ridded me of the nuisance, I could never have done him (ergo, his dog) any good.

Some sad tales do have happy endings. This is one. Big Red went on to earn the CD in three consecutive shows with scores in the 190s. More important, his owner—who had since moved to another state—mailed me a quotation that speaks volumes. He'd come across it in a book on horse training and knew of my penchant for such points of wisdom. He credits Xenophon, a Greek calvary general and equine trainer (circa 400 B.C.), with having written:

> If the horse does not enjoy his work, the rider will have no joy. If the rider is not in harmony with the nature of the animal, the animal will perform its tasks as though burdened, with no display of pleasure.

A NOVICE TENDENCY

To lapse in method is common for beginning trainers. For example, at a first-week basic class an owner commands "Sit," pooch sits and the student just stands there, staring at the animal, clueless about what to do next. This, despite the fact that everyone had been told moments before to praise "Good sit" when their dogs complied.

A student/friend helped me to see the reason for this phenomenon. "Joel, you've forgotten how dumbstruck a person can be the first time he sees that his dog can learn and will be obedient. An owner's momentary, 'Well, I'll be!' reaction causes him to forget to follow through with praise."

I've been indebted to this perceptive young man ever since. As mentioned in the Preface, "You may be surprised at the quality and quantity of lessons students and their dogs can teach you."

A monumental lesson? No. An important one? You bet.

OH, REALLY?

"Old people like that got no bidness trying to train a dog," or so an acquaintance muttered shortly before a first-week novice class as we watched a lady of advanced years being leash-pulled through the doorway by a young, headstrong Beagle.

"As much business as anyone else," I rejoined. The man just shook his head and continued completing an enrollment form.

The weeks went by, the lady gradually brought her Beagle into line, and by the final class my reading was that she and her pet had done very well. In fact, they had accomplished more than most and significantly more than had my acquaintance who had originally critically commented on her "bidness," an ironic point that wasn't lost on him.

True, you may have to intervene if a seasoned senior—or anyone else—is being dragged about by an exuberant behemoth he or she can't control. That situation is discussed in chapter 8, "Just Before a First-Week Class." In such instances, however, I've seldom found the student's age to be a deciding factor. More often the difficulties are related to the person's coordination, agility, strength and—perhaps most important—attitude.

STUBBORN OR DISPIRITED?

As you see, *Teaching Obedience Classes and Seminars* is a teaching guide, not a training manual. Still, I wish to illustrate one aspect of training as I've witnessed no small amount of misunderstanding about the technique. How to apply it isn't the problem. The issues are: When is it proper and with which types of dogs is it effective?

My first class consisted of one student. The dog was a Labrador Retriever named Muldoon. Although we were in the throes of a nasty Wyoming winter at the time, desperation in the caller's voice led me to work singly with him and his pet. It developed that the Lab was truly in a class by himself as he was about as stubborn as members of this breed get.

As is my custom I began the team's education by demonstrating how to teach, "Sit." The dog resisted but, given my method of teaching the exercise, obstinacy to the lesson is easily overcome. The real problem occurred when we progressed to heeling. Regardless of inducements, Muldoon wouldn't budge, save to lie down and say, "Make me!"

"Carl," I told the owner, "Give the command once more, pat your leg again, then turn your back and get to walking."

Carl did as instructed. The Lab protested with great indignation at being dragged through the snow, but before Carl had taken six steps Muldoon hopped up, joined his owner and, as the gentleman later commented, "He's been like glue on my left leg ever since."

This dragging bit is a fallback technique of which I've never been fond. I've used it no more than a dozen times over the years, and only when the animal radiated pure defiance and I was sure his spirit wouldn't be at risk, that he was mentally tough enough to take what he was dishing out without crumbling.[2]

Of course, spirit is why the method works. Muldoon didn't relent from pain or fear but from offended senses of pride and self-worth. My use of "great indignation" in describing the Lab's reaction is bull's-eye accurate. It's why the dog hopped up after just a few steps (in fact, if the animal doesn't get on his paws within six or seven steps the handler should stop; the method isn't going to work). Applying the technique to an apathetic rather than super-stubborn dog is not only ineffective, it reinforces withdrawn behavior.

Along with a few Muldoons, you're going to meet some Sunshines, Roscoes and Boychicks. Those are some of the few dogs I've encountered who gave heightened meaning to the word indifferent. Often puppy-mill products, these animals either arrived on the planet bereft of spirit or had their souls shattered by circumstance. They are the ones for whom force confirms their feelings of worthlessness, not an avoidable, self-wrought consequence.

WHAT YOU TEACH IS WHAT YOU GET

I relate the following during novice classes and seminars. It's presented in monologue form to illustrate how I impart the story.

I remember a novice student who could unleash a voice that imperiled all glass objects within a several-block radius. The good news was she only tuned up when perturbed. The bad news was she became perturbed easily.

The lady had a highly trainable German Shepherd who was as willing as he was bright. During a third-week novice class I asked the students to "Platz" their dogs so I could see how everyone had fared with the previous week's lesson. Everything was fine until the Shepherd decided that Platz wasn't high on his list of things to do that afternoon, or so it seemed.

The owner moved her dog a few feet and said "Sit." The dog sat. The lady commanded "Platz" but the animal remained sitting. So the owner again said "Platz," louder this time. Pooch continued to sit but a few students had heard the decibel increase and had begun to watch.

The third "Platz" had the attention of the entire class, along with that of some of my neighbors, and I began to wish I had an earplug concession. The owner, now thoroughly perturbed, bellowed "Dammit! Platz!" and yanked her leash earthward. The dog dropped, beating the correction to the ground, and I found myself thinking, "I wonder . . ."

---

[2]The technique should never be used on rough surfaces, like blacktop or concrete, but only in snow, soft dirt or on lawns.

I approached the team and asked if I might work the dog a moment. Exasperated, the lady said "Sure" and I moved the animal a few feet away.

At this point I'm patting my left leg and saying "C'mon, dog," as though I'm walking a canine while staring toward the imaginary animal. After a few steps I tell the invisible critter "Sit." Next I praise "Good sit" while pantomiming petting the dog.

Then I stand erect, command "Dammit!" and follow the unseen dog's drop with a downward jerk of my head. By now the listeners are chuckling. As I bend over and pet the illusionary German Shepherd, I praise "Gooood dammit" and the group comes to full roar. As the laughter subsides I speak to the class.

The message, of course, is how easy it is to confuse a willing dog. I mean, the animal sat when told to, and when he heard the command to "Dammit," he went to ground as if a thousand bricks had fallen upon him. That isn't the mark of a resistant canine but a misguided one.

Often someone asks if we changed the command.

Nope. The owner said she wanted to keep it, as a reminder to herself.

Summary: This is the kind of training blunder that you or I would never make. But we have to keep in mind that students are just that—students, not trainers. They can make a "Dammit" mistake and not even know they've erred.

THE PEST

During a seminar I was challenged by a local instructor whose months of experience entailed having trained two dogs to iffy levels of reliability. The gentle six-month-old Cocker I was teaching to lie down had submissively rolled over. Seeing I had knelt next to the pupper and was rubbing her gut, the instructor commented smugly, "Doesn't what you're doing constitute positive reinforcement for it to roll over?"

Dogs seldom vex me like some people do, especially captious ones. I was tempted to reply, "If you want to heckle go to a night club," but I settled for, "Of course not."

First, in my perception of things canine, a dog is not an *it*. Most objects and some people are, but not dogs. Second, a half-baked comprehension of any concept is incomplete by definition. Contextually I'm referencing human psychological concepts being misapplied to and unaccompanied by knowledge about another species.

The instructor felt I should have rejected the Cocker's "I accept your domination" message by flipping her into the on-paws posture. That's a demoralizing approach, one that could have negated the rapport the animal and I were developing. Such harshness could have said "Not good enough!" to a young dog who was giving her best. Besides, as I knew she would, the pup rolled into the ideal position when and because I stood. My movement suggested I might leave, and she was already sufficiently attracted to me to want to be ready to tag along.

"YOU'VE GOT TO BE KIDDING!"

That's what I said when the instructor told me that she didn't know the first thing about dogs, how they learn, what motivates them. She continued, "I've trained a few of my own dogs, and I read a [how-to-teach-classes] book, committed parts of it to memory and hung out my shingle."

"So tell me," I said, "What do you do when there's a problem? When one-size-fits-all training doesn't work?"

"I've never had such a problem."

I translated that to mean she'd never recognized trouble, like a learning difficulty, when it was staring her in the face.

"I've had to handle a few aggressive dogs," she went on, "and some real stubborn ones, but I just hung them like another book said to do until they decided they'd had enough."

Message: You will probably encounter some dolts in this business. Try not to let them get to you.

DAY-MAKER

The Cockapoo's name was Ginger. Her new owner had, "found her at the pound but they were going to put her down because she was pregnant. Finally, after a lot of phone calls between them and me and the vet, they let me have her." Weeks later Ginger's owner helped her deliver two breech-birth pups, found homes for the little ones, and Ginger's life seemed on the upswing.

But the adorable little animal must have done something terribly wicked in a previous incarnation: Some months before her second birthday, Ginger went blind. Not partially, pitch black.

Even a blind dog can be successfully taught a wide range of useful behaviors.

Now, we've all known people who would have reflexively opted for euthanasia. As in, "I just don't have time." As in, "Forget yesterday's promises—everything's different now." As in, "Who needs a dog that can't see?"

How did Ginger's owner respond? By calling me and asking, "Can we take your class?" As the lady told me, "I want to help Ginger's confidence."

Heeling, sit, stay and the like can be learned by a blind dog, of course, but that isn't the point. Neither is the fact that I had to modify some of my teaching/training techniques and objectives. That's just technical stuff. The lesson here is, well, I'll let you draw your own conclusions. Moments ago I called Ginger's owner. "I need to ask you something," I told her, "and I hope you won't take it wrong. When you learned Ginger was losing her sight, why did you decide to keep her?"

"What else was I going to do with her?" the lady responded, taken somewhat aback, "I mean, she's my dog."

Day-maker.

LOOK OUT, EXPERT!

The following first appeared in *Kennels and Kenneling.* It's included here given the tale's relevance to this book's subject matter.

Occasionally you may be asked to evaluate a dog. Though your initial impulses may be helpfulness and promoting your services, be careful. Be very, very careful.

The Doberman seemed aloof but otherwise friendly enough as he leash-pulled his owner into my training yard. The man had phoned earlier, asking if I would help him find a home for the dog. I receive many such calls, as well as contacts from folks wanting to acquire a pet, and my practice is to record the person's name and phone number in hope that I'll hear of a match. Something in this caller's tone caught my attention, however, and though it's not my usual practice, I asked that he bring the dog by for a once-over.

Owner and dog arrived. Soon I was on one knee in front of and inches to the dog's right, caressing the back of his neck with my left hand while my right hand was near the left-center of his chest. The Dobe was enjoying the contact. All was well.

Suddenly the dog went rigid. His breathing stopped, his pupils expanded, he attacked me. I don't mean he nipped in my direction—he detonated: Full-mouth shots and intense growling.

I'd learned long ago that the safest course when besieged is to move no more than absolutely necessary. Get what anatomy you must out of harm's way, yes, but use as little movement as possible. The reason for this is akin to the notion of not running when near a swarm of bees or hornets: Swift motion can excite and attract the insects. My reflexes took over—there was no time for conscious thought—and I was spared injury.

To this day I can mentally replay the incident in slow motion with vivid detail and clarity. The Doberman's initial assault was toward my face. I snapped my head back just far enough that he lost interest and redirected toward the faster motion of my left hand, which I was rapidly moving up and away from the dog, knowing at a subliminal level that doing so would cause him to target it next and that he would not be able to reach it.

But it was close. It was very close. I felt the dog's whiskers brush my cheek as he changed direction toward my hand. As his jaws snapped shut, his muzzle hairs grazed the palm of my raised hand. Just then the leash tightened, preventing further advance.

At no time did I stand. That takes too long and had I done so, the animal would likely have reacted by nailing me in a leg. How long did the event last? Maybe three seconds, certainly no more than that. Did I see the attack coming? Yes, but only a blink before it began. Nothing in the dog's aspect had even hinted at hostility before then.

My purpose in relating this tale is to illustrate two dangers inherent in dealing with unknown canines. The first is obvious: Dogs can unjustly and without provocation launch an all-out war in a flicker. They have the ability to switch from relative dormancy to full-on and flat-out in less time than it would take the average person to raise his hands in defense.

The second risk is less obvious: In a situation like this, don't expect any help from the owner. You may have noticed that I didn't tell you that the man "hurriedly pulled his dog back." That's because he didn't. My full attention was on the Doberman, you understand, but I was aware that the owner didn't move a muscle. He just stood there with his mouth hanging open, watching the show. Nor did he advise me ahead of time that the dog had, without apparent cause, attacked several people in similar fashion, though I later learned from other sources that the animal had done just that.

Is this event typical of my daily life as a dog trainer? No, thank God. Such events are very rare. So why have I told you about such an isolated incident? Because you work with dogs; because you need to know what can happen; and because in such circumstances, infrequent though they may be, all it may take is once to cause you serious injury. Better you should learn prudence from my experience than from personal calamity.

When dealing with dogs you don't know, "be very, very careful."

GIVE THEM ENOUGH ROPE . . .

This one happened to a friend in a Midwestern state. I have her permission to tell you about it.

Ann (not her real name) had moved to a town dominated in training by one kennel club and one private trainer. The club had held sway for years, was hung up on structuring its eight-week series along the CD routine, and thought nothing of enrolling forty to fifty students in a single class. The private trainer was an incompetent whose ad proclaimed him a "certified trainer," notwithstanding his diploma came from a mill offering certificates to anyone who'd pony up an outlandish sum for its few-weeks course.

In the face of all this, Ann began offering classes. Before too long, the result of a pet shop who believed in and promoted her, along with word of mouth from satisfied students and sound business practices, she owned the town trainingwise.

The kennel club's leadership reacted by promptly bringing in a pseudo hotshot for an "Open to the Public" clinic. I understand they didn't take it too well when no one signed up. Truly, not one person enrolled and the seminar had to be canceled.

So the club spent a considerable sum advertising its upcoming classes. Accustomed to heavy turnouts, the powers that be were mortified to enroll just seven students, all club members, not incidentally.

The private trainer one-upped the club. Though he would have been well advised to take Ann's classes and try to learn something about dogs and training, he convinced an accomplice to enroll, learn all she could and report back. The plan was that together they would then use Ann's training and business techniques to pump up their dwindling enrollments.

Of course, that didn't work either. Ann's success sprung from her training and dog knowledge and rapport with people, and from the fact that she dealt from confidence, not fear. Her goal was to establish a successful training service, not to put others out of business. As she recently told me, "Given their screws are in urgent need of tightening, and that they lack maturity and professionalism, they'll do themselves in without any help from me."

Message: Quality still sells. If you teach classes in a heavily contested area, don't worry if competitors panic. That's their problem, and the implication is that they're worried, probably with good reason. As far as spies go, chuckle to yourself as you deposit their checks. Every time you run a series you're demonstrating how to teach, but the reality is no one can copy you. Your teaching style is as much a function of your personality and philosophy as it is of your knowledge and experience. No one can do it like you.

Incidentally, in telling me about all this, Ann passed along a quotation. Taken from a serious book that deals in part with the Civil War, the lines had a nonserious, chuckle-producing effect upon us both, given Ann's situation. I hope you enjoy the excerpt, too.

> "No matter what the other side does to you, you grin and walk through the cannon smoke. It drives them crazy."[3]

DOG SHOPPING

Because you're more knowledgeable about dogs than the average person, you may be asked for occasional help about selecting a breed or type of dog. Some years ago a friend of mine, a frail, older lady who used a walker, sought my assistance. Time had not tamed her tongue, however, for when she told me that she planned to acquire a four-year-old male Great Dane, having had Danes as a girl, and, "To hell with what that (adjective removed) nephew of mine says about it!" the lady and I, shall we say, exchanged views.

I knew the dog. He was being given away, and with good reason: He was very dominant and more than slightly cantankerous toward other dogs and human authority. He wasn't vicious, but was what is generally meant by the term *bad actor.* When I tried to point all this out to my friend, in hopes that she'd see that this was not the dog for her, she demanded, "McMains, what the hell do you know?"

"I know that dog," I told her, "and that he could snap your bones like kindling, an action that might be to his liking." We glared at one another for a bit, she said she'd think about it, and, days later, met me halfway by dragging me off to a breeder who was selling a two-year-old male Irish Wolfhound who was as laid-back as the breed gets.

---

[3]James Lee Burke, *In the Electric Mist with Confederate Dead* (New York: Avon, 1993), 214.

"He's nice," I agreed, after spending some time with the dog, "but could you lift him into your car if you had to, like in an emergency?"

"Do you know anyone who could?" she shot back. I shut up.

She took the dog through my classes, and today has a loyal, loving, obedient companion who worships his owner. Moral: When helping someone decide about a dog, put temperament and character first, and realize that size match-ups are not only but one consideration, they're relative, too.

ALL TEETH AND SPIT

Never during my classes and seminars had there been a dog I could not approach. Some required a hefty degree of caution but I've never had to back away.

Then I met a year-old White Bull Terrier crossbreed named Klotzy. He and his owner walked in to a first-week class, Klotzy took one bug-eyed look at the other dogs and people, and full-lunged to the end of the leash, manifesting as much fear-driven aggression as I'd ever seen.

Using various "tricks" for dealing with canine hostility I tried to settle the animal but soon abandoned the effort. My concern was he might feel so cornered as to wheel around and try to take his owner. She had her hands full, appeared more than a trifle worried, and—heels dug in—was doing well to restrain her pet.

My initial thought was to give up on the dog but four things kept me hanging in there. One was that I'd never met a critter like Klotzy and I was curious. Another was the owner's assurance that, "He's like this only around strangers, never with people he knows." Motivations three and four were the lady's obvious feelings for her pet and her common sense in not trying to console the out-of-control animal. Many novices would have reflexively done that and such reassurance, of course, would have had the effect of cheering the dog on.

I agreed to meet privately with the owner but I had more than a few misgivings about the outcome. Klotzy was one fast, powerful dog, and after his formidable display of, "Keep your distance!" I was operating more on hope than certitude.

In any event, I *knew* Klotzy could never be allowed to return to class. He was just too dangerous. Besides, no tyro trainer would ever be able to turn such a dog around to that degree. The lady might achieve some cosmetic obedience—and, to my mind, even that was iffy—but infuse enough reliability to return to class safely? Nope. Out of the question. Just not possible. Never happen. Right?

Wrong.

Klotzy came back three weeks later. As students watched in open-mouthed amazement, one gentleman in particular muttering, "That *can't* be the same dog!," the animal's youthful master smoothly moved him through his paces. I approached the team, petted Klotzy and congratulated the lady who trained him.

The students asked one common question that evening, and made one recurring observation. The question was, "How'd she do it?" The observation: "Joel, your training really did something there." That last implied a truth of a kind and I told the group as much, answering the question in the process.

My techniques contributed to Klotzy's turnaround, yes, but they didn't cause it. They opened a door to the animal through which the owner could reach him. What she communicated was her belief in her pet and their bond, that together they could handle anything, that his fear could be put in the trash can where it belonged. Klotzy heard her and trusted her. That's what turned him around.

As I laptop this account, having been invited to the student's house for supper, Klotzy is curled up next to me on the couch, sound asleep, and I'm at full grin. Not just in satisfaction over the dog's adjustment per se, but in the long-range implications. You see, what I haven't told you is Klotzy's owner felt that if he couldn't be trained he'd have to be put down.

In that sense this account is symbolic. No, Klotzy's behavior isn't common—hardly—but variations on it are. Many an owner has told me, in effect, "Either we get a handle on this dog or he's through." Almost always we "get a handle" on the animal in question and the result is that a former problem dog has a home for life. For a professional trainer, being able to contribute to such outcomes is satisfying—very, very satisfying.

BIAS

"What a worker!" That was the consensus as the Rotty hopped over the jump, raced toward her owner and, after an exuberant finish, heeled with animated precision back to the group.

"Oh, how cute!" That was the consensus as the Miniature Dachshund hopped over the jump, raced toward his owner and, after an exuberant finish, heeled with animated precision back to the group.

As these were the last two dogs for the recall-over-high jump exercise, everyone looked toward me to see what we'd do next. Knowing that silence can sometimes capture more attention than a loudspeaker, and feeling that what I was about to say might be my most important offering during the five-week interme-diate series, I remained silent for several seconds. Then I walked to the Rottweiler, petted her and said, "You did great." I approached the Miniature Dachshund, petted him and said, "So did you." Both animals seemed to understand. Now if I could get it across to the class.

Tasha and Blackjack were really "on" tonight, yes?

Lots of smiles and even some applause as students looked first at one dog then the other.

You bet they were. In fact, all the dogs have been doing well this evening, have they not?

Sounds of affirmation, more smiles, students petting their dogs. So far so good.

I heard several comments about Tasha being a heck of a worker. You won't get an argument out of me. She is impressive.

Several nods, and the first stirrings of curiosity. Some of these people knew me too well; they could tell when I was leading up to something.

And Blackjack, he's a fireball, too. Agreed?

A chorus of, "He sure is!"

One question: How come Tasha's a "worker" while Blackjack's "cute"?

Silence. Then, "Well," a student began, "Tasha's a big dog, and Blackjack's so tiny, so . . . cute, adorable."

Tasha's not adorable? You might want to check with her owner about that.

Laughter.

I remember a student who owned a Pomeranian whom he often referred to as "Killer," though that wasn't her name. What does that say to you?

"Making fun of the dog," someone responded, a sentiment the group shared.

Do you see where I'm going with this?

"I do and I appreciate it," Blackjack's owner piped up. "My dog's cute, sure, but he's working his butt off too, just as hard as Tasha is. The work's just as hard for him as for any dog."

Amen. A Miniature Dachshund can't stride like a Rottweiler. Not physically, he can't. His anatomy won't allow it. But in his heart he can. And does.

Nods and chuckles.

I know that no one was poking fun at Blackjack. You guys are taken with him like I am. But I also know the working efforts of small dogs are sometimes perceived with less than total objectivity. That not only deprives the animal of the respect he or she deserves, it limits the viewer's awareness. And when a group mentally pooh-poohs a dog's efforts, the critter can receive the message and his attitude can go down. Think on it.

"A LAB WHO WON'T JUMP?"

That's what ran through my mind as Alec froze in front of the jump. His owner had left him on a sit-stay, stepped over the eight-inch-high jump and called him. Alec took a hesitant step or two toward the hurdle, froze, lowered his head and began to shiver.

All this took place during an intermediate class. The dog had done well in basic Obedience, the over-jump-at-heel and recall lessons had presented no problem for him, we were using the same jump, so I had expected the year-old Labrador to recall-hop over the obstacle as most of his breed would.

But Alec wasn't having any part of it. I called a halt to the proceedings and asked the class, "What's the problem here?"

Consensus: The dog was afraid.

"Why?" I asked.

"Something about the jump," everyone agreed.

"What?" was my third question. No one had an answer, me included.

People, I've no earthly notion why Alec's afraid but he obviously is. What should we do?

A student suggested that having the owner lift Alec over the jump might help, "like I did when my dog balked during the over-jump-at-heel training in the beginner class. That solved the problem for her."

The owner tried it but the problem remained. Alec accepted being lifted over the obstacle—he didn't flail about or the like—but he still wouldn't recall over the board.

OK, now what? We could just skip this exercise with Alec but I don't think we're to that point. What else might we try?

No response.

Alright, let me ask you something. Is there a dog here who enjoys verbal praise more than Alec?

The group agreed there wasn't. More than one student had commented on how much the Labrador enjoyed hearing his name and being told how well he was doing a given exercise. With that happy thought in mind I asked the students to form an eight-foot-wide corridor centered along an imaginary line leading to the jump. Then I spoke to the owner and the group.

Now bring Alec to the middle of the corridor and sit him about four feet from the jump. After you command "Stay" and step over the jump to its other side, call him. I imagine he'll start toward you as he did earlier. Just as he takes that first step I want everyone to begin clapping and cheering, "Good Alec!" over and over. If he goes across the board, clap and cheer louder. Everyone got the idea?

They did. The owner called Alec, he took a step, the group responded as instructed, Alec was still nervous but he kept going and stepped over the board.

OK, quickly now, before he loses his nerve, bring Alec back to the starting point and run the sequence again.

By the fourth repetition Alec's head was up and his tail was up as he leaped over the board.

Moral: Just as a class's belittlement of Blackjack's efforts can negatively affect the dog's spirit, before-the-fact praise intensified by a group is a powerful tool. It can override a dog's nervousness to the extent that he has a chance to see there's nothing to fear in what is being asked of him.

OBLIGATIONS, MORAL AND LEGAL

The owner was drunk. I'd caught whiffs of the liquor on his breath at previous meetings but today he'd arrived at class fully besotted. I also suspected he'd taken additional fortification during a couple of "be right back" trips to his car.

A problem for me? Not really. We were four weeks into the series and the guy's dog was doing reasonably well, save for periodic confusion that I attributed to erratic training practices, inconsistent behavior being typical of alcoholics. Fortunately, the owner was a cheery drinker; I didn't have to worry about keeping him off his dog when things didn't go right, as can be the case when demon rum causes the user to become a "mean" drunk.

My dilemma started when the class ended for the day. Had the man caused an accident during his trek home I might have been legally vulnerable. Of a certainty, I would have felt morally out of tune.

So what to do? This is one of those instances where it would be presumptuous for me to suggest what you should do. I can only relate what I did. I sought out the man—we'll call him John—and eased him away from the other departing students.

"John, could I have a word with you over here?"

"Sure, wha's up?"

"John, you're not in a condition to drive safely. You know why as well as I do. Can you call for a ride?"

Pause.

"Now, you look here. . . ."

"No, John, you look. I'm in a spot that's not of my making. I could look the other way but that's not just unfair to you and your dog, it ignores the folks you might plow into."

"I can drive. . . ."

"Not safely, you can't. Now, you have a choice: You can call for a ride or—if you get in your car—I'll call the cops. They'll have you before you get ten blocks and you can discuss the unfairness of it all with them. Which will it be?"

John called for a ride. Directly his wife arrived and collected him and I never saw the man again, much to my relief. He did phone once, asking for his money back, but I refused the request. I figured I had more than earned my fee.

Sure, this is one of the more off-the-wall negatives attendant to working with the public, but someday you may be faced with a similar situation. Better you consider now how you might handle it.

SUBTLETY

Skipper was a year-old Golden. To say that he was trainable was like saying Babe Ruth had a flair for baseball. However, Skipper was also quite sensitive, as you'll see.

The novice class had progressed to fifteen-foot, on-leash recalls when Skipper's owner, Tim, a first-time trainer who had the touch and needed only experience, reported a problem: The dog's front sits were starting to go crooked. The animal was no longer plunking his rear at high noon but at about ten o'clock. Most owners would neither notice nor care about such a slight deviation but Tim already had his eyes on the CD degree.

Now, if you'd care to solve this one as you read along, you need to know that Skipper was being trained on a small-link pinch collar and that the class had worked on heeling just before we commenced recall practice. Also, be aware that during a recall the Golden looked down and to his right just before sitting in front of his trainer.

"Where's the problem?" I asked Tim.

"Skipper's sitting a bit crooked," he answered.

"I know, but at what end of the dog is the problem originating?"

"Well, the rear," Tim responded, somewhat taken aback that I'd asked a question having such a seemingly obvious answer.

"You sure?" I said.

Thoughtful silence.

"Let me recall Skipper a few times," I offered. "Stand a bit behind me and off to my left side. Watch the dog closely. Then we'll talk about what you saw."

Tim agreed and I proceeded to recall the Golden a few times. Skipper continued to sit somewhat crooked.

"I see he glances to his right just before he sits," Tim observed.

"Good. At what?" I asked.

Tim didn't have an answer. Frankly, I'd have been surprised if he had. As mentioned earlier, the young man was new to training. I told him:

The problem is at the front end, not the rear. We did some heeling at the start of class today. In the process Skipper's collar got turned on his neck. The chain part, where your leash attaches, is now to the dog's right. The leash's weight exerts just enough pressure that this sensitive critter can feel it. As he sits in front of you he moves his front a hair to his left, away from the weight on the collar. That's what he's been trying to see when he's glanced to his right: Where the pressure was coming from. Moving his front to the left causes his rear to shift a bit to his right. Result: a crooked sit. Reposition the collar so that the chain is under his jaw, and attach your lead to both rings, so the collar can't close at all. Then recall Skipper and see what happens.

Tim did as instructed. Skipper recalled four times and sat arrow straight each time. For the next few minutes Tim looked at me like I'd just arrived from Mars, and muttered "My God!" a lot.

There's no great moral in this account, save the obvious: An instructor has to be able to hear what a dog is saying. Otherwise, the tale is presented only as a technical study in problem solving.

OUCH!

The instructor was a paradox: a cocky young gent yet one of those folks you couldn't help but like. He had an infectious smile, an earthy sense of humor and his knowledge of dogs and dog training was impressive. The students and dogs at the weekend seminar were very taken with him and the feeling was obviously mutual.

He'd brought along one of his dogs, as responsive a Great Dane as I'd seen. She was reliable, happy, enthusiastic and what I term "Doberman quick" in her movements. I'd been around Danes since my prekindergarten days and could not remember one who responded so swiftly to command.

At one point several dogs were in a line on down-stays. The instructor's Dane was among them, at about the midway point. He was stepping over each dog while speaking to the group. I don't remember his topic but just as he stepped over his Dane he used the word, "Sit."

She sat. That's why this vignette is titled "Ouch!" That isn't precisely what he said—a verbatim quote would never get past my editor—but I can tell you there were numerous references to the Deity.

That evening the instructor and I went out for dinner and, of course, discussion of the event was inevitable. He was still a mite tender and I probably didn't help matters when I asked if he'd ever thought he might be better off with a smaller dog.

"You know," he grinned, "that stepping-over-the-dogs bit is something I've done ever since I saw someone do it years ago. I remember thinking at the time that I didn't like it, that it seemed somehow demeaning to the animals, but I figured this is part of what you do if you're an instructor and I just never questioned it again."

"I expect you're questioning it now," I chuckled.

"Something like this happens," he said, ignoring my wit, "it's like something's trying to get your attention, to tell you something. I think I'll drop walking over dogs from the act."

Some seminars are more educational than others. This one was dynamite.

GRADUATION BLUES

Four of the seminar attendees were AKC-oriented instructors. During a visit after a day's session, first one and then all bewailed that so few students had shown up for graduation. Each also confirmed that they routinely announced during the prior session that graduation would entail a minishow for grading each team. I suggested that they either drop the competition idea, or at least not mention it during the next-to-the-last meeting.

I heard from each of these folks during the following year. Two had eliminated competition graduations, two just quit mentioning it during the preceding class. The rates for people showing up for the final session significantly increased.

As stated in chapter 5, "Teaching Guidelines," "most dog owners are pet owners who have neither the time, interest nor inclination for competition. They want obedience suited to the way they live. Period." A corollary is that competition vis-à-vis the family pet can make some owners so nervous that they'll avoid competitive situations to bypass the anxiety it causes.

LOOK OUT, STUDENT!

The animal was the product of crossing a Great Dane with a Mack truck, or such was my opinion. At six months of age he was still more puppy than dog, but even so possessed more maturity than his teenage owner. Were I to guess I'd opine that the young man had been reared in a sheltered environment, as he was often hesitant to the point of indecision. That's not an indictment, just a clarification.

During a novice-class heeling exercise the dog playfully tried to climb his owner's back. The lad attempted to elbow the dog away but to no avail. "Lean forward, turn left," I shouted, but the young man only continued to flail away. Just then playful turned dangerous as the dog snapped at the back of his owner's neck and the young man's face went white. That's when I ran to him, tore the leash from his hand and told the dog, "We got to have speaks."

I attempted to heel the animal from his handler's location, and pooch responded by lunging at me. I drove a knee into his chest, causing him to jump backward. The dog gathered himself and came back for more. As he did I leash-jerked him upward and toward myself and drove my knee into his brisket, hard. The dog rose about a foot into the air, yelped, and the dust began to settle. As my adrenaline level began to normalize I knelt, patted my leg and entreated the animal's puppy aspect to, "C'mere." He did. He'd gotten his mind right. I petted him and got my face washed. I visited with the owner about what had just taken place, accenting that he needed to work on being in charge.

Moral: Just as I told you in "Look Out, Expert!," above, don't expect any help from an owner if a dog tries to attack you, don't expect a targeted student to react properly. Immediately intervene, because in a high-stress situation your instructions, no matter how concisely put, may go unheeded. The person may not even hear you.

TO PLATZ THE BISMARCK!

A medium-sized crossbreed of indeterminate origin, Bismarck not only refused to lie down, he resisted to the point of snapping at his owner when the man tried to force the dog to ground.

"Does he snap at you at home?" I asked.

"Never. And at home he lies down without a problem."

OK, group, put on your think-dog caps. Bis willingly downs at home. He's doing everything else commanded of him here. It's a fourth-week class so he knows all the dogs present, they aren't a problem for him. Other than a few zillion leaves drifting around this fall day we have no distractions to speak of. What's Bismarck's problem?

I'd offered a clue but no one picked up on it. The only sound was the slight breeze whispering through the trees at the college campus where the class was being held.

C'mon, folks. He never resists "Platz" at home. What's going on here?

No reply.

Ed, tell Bismarck to sit and then to lie down. Command him just once and don't force the issue if he doesn't hit the ground. Everyone else, watch the dog's reaction. Go for it, Ed.

Ed commanded Bismarck to sit, he sat, and then to Platz. As before, the dog riveted his attention on the ground in front of him, opened his mouth, stood and stepped backward a pace.

"Why, he seems afraid," a lady observed.

Of what?

"I don't know," she answered.

No one else could take it further, which, frankly, would have been surprising. Remember, this was a novice class.

Let me show you something. Ed, heel Bismarck ten or fifteen feet away from where you're standing, in any direction you want.

Then I walked to the spot where Bis had refused to lie down and started shoeing a three-foot-square area free of leaves.

Ed, bring Bismarck back over here. Have him sit on this patch of bare ground I've uncovered, then command him to Platz.

He did, the dog Platzed as through there'd never been a problem, and the class responded with chuckles and a couple of "I'll be damned!"

Ed, I've never been to your house but I bet you don't have a lot of leaves on the ground where you train.

"Sure don't."

People, do you remember my telling you weeks ago that dogs naturally turn in place several times before lying down, because nature tells them to flatten grass and look for snakes and such? Well, what you saw this afternoon is just another manifestation of that instinct. Ed was telling Bis one thing, nature was whispering another. In time the animal may listen more to Ed, but this dog has had only a few weeks of training.

We've all known "trainers" who would have slammed a Bismarck to the ground in the name of "Dogs must mind!" And while it's true that mind they must, it's equally true that fear-based obedience doesn't get it.

OOPS!

The clinic instructor was a bit aloof but innocuous enough, or so I thought until he scuttled his own ship. Toward the end of the final session, while grinning like the fabled Cheshire, he allowed that, "Periodically we all encounter a class of goofballs."

Many in the group gasped, others struggled to maintain a straight face. The guy had just shot himself in the foot.

"Thank you," a student said, her voice laced with sarcasm.

After two or three seconds of realization, the lecturer hurriedly tried to recover. "Oh, no, no, no. I wasn't referring to you people. I was talking about your students."

Too late. And too frail. All the backpedaling in the world couldn't help him now. True, he hadn't been knocking any of us, but a case of the cutes via his unfortunate choice of language had led him to dig a hole; and as fast as he tried to crawl out of it, he dug it deeper.

"Well, I didn't care for such comments about my students, either," someone else in the audience stated in a tone that would chill a penguin.

How to bomb a seminar in six seconds could be this story's title. That's about how long it took, and although the clinic had been pretty good up to this point, the last hour was going to be strained at best. The teacher had walled-off the students.

Sure, you see where he was going: Some people are difficult to reach, to educate, and sometimes they show up en masse. That's just a matter of statistics.

But aloofness is self-imposed distance, and any type of distance can hinder communication. That, and folks who tend to look down their nose can get their eyes crossed in the process, and we both know how that affects perception. While I don't imagine these insights are apocalyptic, feelings of superiority, however unfounded, can be self-defeating, especially for instructors.

No one likes being laughed at, directly or by proxy. Too, some of us withstand shots taken at ourselves better than we accept derision focused upon people not present to defend themselves. Witness the lady who "didn't care for such comments about my students."

No one seeks out an Obedience class for the purpose of being stereotyped or ridiculed. Every person, every dog, every class is different, and each should be responded to in kind. People driven to judge others risk missing out on a great deal as they seldom see past the labels they affix on others.

In any case, if the instructor had ever read this chapter's closing quotation, its veracity may have been lost on him.

BETWIXT THIS, THAT OR THE OTHER

Some years ago I had to make a career choice: computers, cops or canines? Knowing that infinitely higher frustration can be obtained from disks and detecting than dogs, I chose the latter.

The money's better in computers but the return is less. Law enforcement has its rewards but its routines, regulations and restrictions can numb the mind. That, and there's always the off chance that some idiot might take a potshot at you.

Anyway, I didn't reach my decision through a process of elimination. The truth is I had to surrender lesser joys for a greater one. "Had to?" one might ask, and "had to" is my answer. I could never turn away from the dogs.

REFLECTION

The secret of education lies in respecting the pupil.

—EMERSON

Postscript

I hope you've enjoyed *Teaching Obedience Classes and Seminars,* and that it will help you develop and refine your own teaching style. It's important that you do: Growth calls to all life while slavish mimicry contributes nothing, to our art or our students, two- and four-legged alike.

Of course, there are risks in going your own way. As John Steinbeck wrote in *East of Eden,* "People like you to be something, preferably what they are." The allure of the herd's approval is that it seems to offer security, but in truth it's a false refuge, assuring only mediocrity. Sure, we all need to try to get along; but adopting the ways of the chameleon is a sellout that honors no one. Moreover, it violates a trust.

Earlier I borrowed from Max Ehrmann's *Desiderata.* Dipping into that same well, "Enjoy your achievements as well as your plans. Keep interested in your own career, however humble; it is a real possession in the changing fortunes of time." Your training, teaching and dog knowledge are sentences comprising "My Career," a chapter in the book being written that is you. Your work is of great value, to yourself as well as to your students and their pets.

Teach owners that—while it's permissible, even desirable, for them to make their pets mind—it's also okay to remember that dogs *are* our best friends, and that most dogs are cooperative and willing by nature, needing only direction; but that no dog should been seen as something of a furry robot, and that his spirit has the right to endure.

Provide useful lessons that coincide with owner needs and maintain a positive outlook with regard to each team's efforts. Remember, you're offering attitudes about the human-canine relationship first and specific lessons second.

And listen. Never forsake the ability to listen.

Glossary

Because the following definitions pertain to Obedience-class instruction, dog training and related concepts, some bear scant resemblance to those in a general English-language dictionary. Descriptions have been kept as nontechnical as possible.

Active resistance   Overt canine defiance of a trainer's intent.

AKC (American Kennel Club)   A governing body whose primary responsibility is maintenance of purebred canine bloodlines in the United States.

Alpha   Pack leader; number-one animal; the boss.

Animation   Overt canine enjoyment.

Anthropomorphism   Assigning human traits and values to another species. This often occurs by comparing dog training to child rearing.

Anticipation   Execution of a command before it's given.

Attitude   Canine behavior revealing the animal's feeling about a command's directive, a situation or an event.

Attraction   Level of canine interest and trust in a handler.

Automatic sit   An obedience basic requiring a dog to sit because an event occurs: During heeling, the handler stops walking; during a recall or retrieve, the animal arrives in front of and facing the handler.

Backsliding   A short-lived phenomenon whereby a dog seems to have forgotten most lessons to date.

Bonding   A process that leads a dog to feel deep attraction toward another animal, canine or human.

Burned-out   Refers to a dog whose training has been so prolonged and repetitious that he's lost interest in the work and may have developed an aversion toward it and the trainer.

Carryover effect   The positive or negative influence upon canine perception of one activity by another.

Challenge the dog   A method that attempts to bring out a dog's best efforts by making tasks just difficult enough that he must work to perform them.

Choke collar   A training collar, commonly fashioned from steel links, that can restrict and even terminate breathing if misused.

Collar tab   A short length of cord or similar material attached to a collar's live ring to provide a quick handle.

Command   A trainer's directive that calls for a dog's response.

Communication   Imparting information, either to humans or dogs.

Companion Dog (CD)   The title for dogs who qualify in the first level of AKC Obedience competition, known as *Novice*.

Companion Dog Excellent (CDX)   The title for dogs who qualify in the second level of AKC Obedience competition, known as *Open*.

Competition   Obedience performed against ideal standards.

Compulsion   Correction; external force; pressure.

Conditioning   Practicing lessons in varying environments.

Consistency   Relating to a dog in an unchanging manner.

Contact   Any form of communication.

Contention   Canine resistance to a trainer's intent.

Correction   Physical and/or verbal pressure applied by a trainer in response to canine disobedience.

Correction match   A fun match that allows ring corrections.

Cue   Synonym for command.

Dead ring   The ring of a training collar to which a trainer does not attach a leash. *See also* Live ring.

Deflection   Ignoring low-risk contention or minor misbehavior to prevent either from escalating.

Desensitization   Altering anxiety-producing responses through gradual exposure to increasingly stressful stimuli.

Distractions   Stimuli that may entice a dog to break from command.

Distraction proofing   Exposing a dog to distractions, the purpose being to teach in a controlled setting that the animal must obey the trainer's commands despite nearby happenings.

Dominance   The stance from which a trainer must operate to secure and maintain the Alpha role.

Dominant   Refers to an animal who would rather lead than follow.

Drive   (1) Behavior that seeks to satisfy instinctual demands. (2) A training technique that capitalizes upon a dog's instincts toward stimuli to which he is attracted. (3) A dog's degree of attraction toward a stimulus.

Exercise   An element of an Obedience repertoire.

Extra-mile principle   A proofing concept that requires more of a dog than the trainer actually wants.

Fear-biter   A dog who reaches the fight-or-flight state with no more provocation than occurs during normal contact situations.

Fear training   A despicable training approach that relies on teaching a dog to respond in order to avoid inhumane pressure.

Fight or flight   Based in defense drive, this is the point in the stress cycle where a dog attempts to either attack or flee the source of stress.

Finish   An Obedience function by which a dog moves on command to the heel position.

Fire   Canine exuberance.

Focus   Directed mental concentration.

Foundational   Refers to an exercise that is valuable not just for its own merits, but which is also a necessary element of a subsequent lesson.

Fun match   A competition event that simulates a formal dog show.

Gender conflict   Refers to a dog who doesn't relate well with humans or canines of the same sex.

Handler   (1) Synonym for trainer. (2) One who shows a dog.

Heeling   Canine synchronous movement with a handler to maintain the heel position.

Heel position   A dog's position at the handler's left side, the animal facing forward, his right shoulder adjacent to the person's left leg.

I and the Not-I   A dog's view of him- or herself in relation to other beings.

Identifiers   Terms that a trainer assigns to objects and beings to create a language beyond commands with his pet.

Independent   A dog who would prefer to be alone and on his own.

Instinct   General inborn urges to act in response to basic needs (survival, pack social structuring, etc.).

Integration   A training phase during which exercises heretofore practiced separately are performed in sequences.

Intelligence   The ability to thrive and problem-solve in any environment.

Learned-helplessness syndrome   Canine acceptance of abuse as an inevitable consequence of contact with humans.

Learning   A permanent behavioral change arising from experience.

Learning rate   The speed at which a dog can absorb new material.

Light lead   A leash appreciably lighter than the primary leash.

Light line   A long, lightweight line used in off-leash training.

Live ring   The ring of a training collar to which a trainer attaches a leash. *See also* Dead ring.

Misdirected anger   Canine ire directed toward a person or object that is not the cause of the animal's resentment.

Moment of recognition   The instant at which a dog's aspect communicates, "Aha! I understand what my trainer wants."

Name   A dog's appellation, which is more of a positively based attention-getter than an identification of self.

Novice   (1) A trainer or dog new to training. (2) *See* Companion Dog.

Open   *See* Companion Dog Excellent.

Ostrich defense   One response of a frightened dog: turning his attention from that which he fears—"If I can't see it, it can't hurt me."

Pack   The social structure of a dog's "family."

Pack leader   *See* Alpha.

Passive resistance   Covert canine opposition to a trainer's intent.

Personality   A dog's habitual manner of relating with his environment and individuals he contacts.

Pinch collar   A multilinked training device which imparts the sensation of teeth grasping the dog's neck.

Playtoy   A toy to which a dog is greatly attracted.

Playwork   A concentration-building exercise rooted in positive-reinforcement techniques.

Praise   Affirmation; approval; communicating to a dog that his behavior is as commanded.

Pressure   Synonym for correction.

Put down   Canine euthanasia.

Rapport   An intangible that says, "I seek that which I project: respect and oneness."

Recall   Summoning a dog to a sitting position in front of and facing the handler.

Reinforcement   A stimulus that can cause a behavior change.

Replacement   A technique used to halt destructive behavior whereby a dog is allowed to vent natural urges acceptably.

Resistance   *See* Active resistance *and* Passive resistance.

Ring nerves   A condition akin to stage fright, often associated with competition.

Ring-wise   (1) A blame-the-dog defense that seeks to transfer responsibility from handler to dog for determining if the animal is ready for competition. (2) Describes a dog who has been shown so many times at a specific competition level that he knows the handler cannot or will not correct in a ring environment.

INDEX

V

W

Y

ABOUT THE AUTHOR

Joel M. McMains, award-winning author for Howell Book House, has been training dogs professionally since "somewhere in the seventies." In addition to offering contract obedience and protection training services, he conducts public obedience classes and training seminars. He served as chief K9 trainer for the Sheridan County (Wyoming) Sheriff's Department and for the city of Sheridan Police Department. Joel has testified in court proceedings as an expert witness, and has taught courses in K9 selection, management, training and deployment for the Police-Science Division of Sheridan College. He was also the coordinator of Sheridan County's 4-H Dog Program from 1982 to 1994. Joel is the author of five books and is a member of the Dog Writers Association of America. He lives near Terre Haute, Indiana.